SPECIAL TEAS

SPECIALTEAS

M. Dalton King

Photography by Katrina De Leon

❁

Prop Styling by Jane Panico-Trzeciak

Food Styling by Marianne S. Twohie

A Running Press/Kenan Book

❁

Running Press
Philadelphia, Pennsylvania

A RUNNING PRESS/KENAN BOOK

Copyright © 1992 by Kenan Books, Inc.

9 8 7 6 5 4 3 2 1

Digit on the right indicates the number of this printing.

Library of Congress Cataloging-in-Publication Number 92-53688

SPECIALTEAS
was prepared and produced by
Kenan Books, Inc.
15 West 26th Street
New York, New York 10010

Editors: Sharon Kalman and Sharyn Rosart
Art Director/Designer: Robert W. Kosturko
Photography Editor: Anne K. Price
Photographs © 1992 Katrina DeLeon
Prop Styling by Jane Panico-Trzeciak
Food Styling by Marianne S. Twohie

Typeset by Classic Type Inc.
Color separations by Colourmatch Graphic Equipment & Services
Printed in Hong Kong by Leefung-Asco Printers Ltd.

This book may be ordered by mail from the publisher.
Please add $2.50 for postage and handling.
But try your bookstore first!

Running Press Book Publishers
125 South Twenty-second Street
Philadelphia, Pennsylvania 19103

Dedicated to Timothy, for keeping the faith.
With special thanks to:
Judie Choate, Dan Green, and Pam Long.

INTRODUCTION ❈ 8

CHAPTER ONE ❈ 10

Tea — The Drink

CHAPTER TWO ❈ 18

House SpecialTeas

CHAPTER THREE ❈ 28

A British Cream Tea

CHAPTER FOUR ❈ 36

An American Cream Tea

CHAPTER FIVE ❈ 42

A Southern Tea

CHAPTER SIX ❈ 50

High Tea

CHAPTER SEVEN ❈ 56

Thanksgiving Tea

CHAPTER EIGHT ❈ 62

Christmas Tea

CHAPTER NINE ❋ 68

EASTER TEA

CHAPTER TEN ❋ 76

RUSSIAN TEA

CHAPTER ELEVEN ❋ 84

CHINESE TEA

CHAPTER TWELVE ❋ 92

CHILDREN'S TEA

CHAPTER THIRTEEN ❋ 100

CHOCOLATE LOVER'S TEA

CHAPTER FOURTEEN ❋ 106

FEEL BETTER TEA

CHAPTER FIFTEEN ❋ 110

LATE-NIGHT TEA

CHAPTER SIXTEEN ❋ 116

BARE BONES TEA

SOURCES ❋ 122

INDEX ❋ 125

INTRODUCTION

WHEN MY PARTNER AND I STARTED TO PUT OUR TEA CATERING SERVICE, SpecialTeas, together, we discovered that there are as many approaches to and ideas about Tea as there are types of tea. Our basic idea was to translate the time-honored British Cream Tea tradition into an American equivalent. We wanted to take the basic idea of Tea and make it suitable for any occasion. Our research showed that this was quite an easy thing to do and has been done for centuries.

Tea is more than lovely cut sandwiches, scones, and delectables. It is an occasion of warmth and sociability between two or more people. It provides the setting for problems to be solved, gossip exchanged, and comfort given.

In initiating SpecialTeas I thought of the many occasions of Tea with friends, some planned and formal, others developed at the spur of the moment. I thought it interesting that the memories of these times were always kind. One in particular kept coming back to me. I was baby-sitting an ill godchild. He had one of those flus children often fall prey to, and was lying bundled on the sofa, feeling small and isolated in his misery. There seemed to be no comfort I could offer him. Juice and ginger ale had lost their appeal. Then I remembered his mother said he could have weak tea with milk and honey. I asked him if he would like to try a "cuppa." A tiny little voice answered yes. I brought him his tea, and as he sat there with the warm cup between his hands and sipped, he began to perk up. He asked for a second cup, but wanted to help make it. While he made the tea I found some saltines. We sat together in the light of the kitchen, sipping, munching, and talking, both of us feeling better. Since that time, whenever we are together, we share a cup of tea.

This atmosphere of shared warmth and camaraderie is what any Tea giver strives for. Unfortunately, many people are a little wary of having Tea. They don't have the familiarity of the everyday to aid them as the British do, thus it becomes an occasion and has the semblance of a mystery. In fact, it's really very easy.

The table you set and the foods you choose are indicators to your guests of the pleasure you receive from their company. The setting can be achieved by using your finest china cups and prettiest linens. Fresh flowers are always lovely. If you have silver, use it, but remember, formal tableware is a plus, not a necessity. A skillful use of the tools at hand will do this nicely. If you are doing a "theme" Tea, use a bit of whimsy. The idea is to establish an atmosphere of conviviality. Think of it as creating a stage for the star of your production—the tea.

That is where this book comes in. The emphasis here is on the food. In putting this service together we decided to use the structure of the British Cream Tea as our model. It is based on a combination of practicality and fun. The sandwiches and tea provide the nourishment, the scones and desserts the fun. Using this three-course meal as a guideline, we have found that it can be adapted to any situation. We provide you with the choices: sandwiches, scones, muffins, biscuits, cakes, and tarts, you make your decisions based on the tastes of you and your guests.

We start out by giving you a good example of a British Tea and then show you how to customize it. We'll show you how to throw a Tea for holidays, children's parties, and for dinner. You'll see that it can be the perfect answer for after the theatre or a late-night "something."

We hope you will come to see Tea as a delight and a wonderful alternative to other types of entertainment. To the British it is a necessity, to us a gift.

M. DALTON KING

CHAPTER ONE

TEA — THE DRINK

A Perfect Pot of Tea

A Perfect Cup of Tea

Iced Tea

Sun-Brewed Iced Tea

Mint Tea Juleps

Lemonade Tea

Serves 6.

TEA FIRST CAME TO THE COLONIES IN AMERICA around 1650 on Dutch ships carrying the "new" drink to the Dutch colony of New Amsterdam. It took another twenty years for the rest of the colonies to become acquainted with tea. Even then, no one really had an idea of how to use it properly. People would let the tea brew and stew for hours, creating a dark, bitter drink. They also salted the used leaves and ate them on buttered bread. It wasn't until 1674, when the British took over New Amsterdam, renaming it New York, that the custom of tea drinking as we now know it was begun.

Prince of Wales Tea: ready for milk, sugar, or lemon.

TYPES OF TEA

Although tea has been sipped in North America for over three centuries, it is much older than that; in fact, over 4,000 years old. And while tea bought at the store is usually a blend of several of the 3,000 varieties available today, there are only three basic types of tea: black, oolong, and green. From these come the blends and varieties.

All tea comes from a single source, an evergreen bush that is a member of the *Camellia sinensis* (tea plant) family. From this bush comes the leaf that is processed into the three types of tea.

BLACK TEA is a completely fermented tea. This is achieved by first oxidizing the leaves, which turns them a beautiful copper color. The leaves are then fired, a process of treating them with blasts of very hot air. Black teas produce the rich, hearty brews popular in this country.

OOLONG TEA is a compromise between black and green teas. It is a partially fermented tea whose leaves are greenish black. The brew produced is lighter in both flavor and color.

GREEN TEA is not oxidized at all. The leaves are steamed after picking to prevent fermentation. These leaves produce a delicate brew that is very light in color. Mothers have used green tea for centuries to help upset stomachs, and there is increasing medical evidence that drinking green tea provides unsuspected health benefits.

Best grown in tropical or subtropical climates at varying altitudes, teas are often named after the region in which

they are grown, such as Assam or Ceylon. Tea leaves are either used singly or mixed with other leaves to form a blend. The combinations are endless. Some of the better known teas and blends are as follows:

BLACK TEAS

Assam: Grown in Northeast India, usually in low altitudes. It is most often used in blends. Rich in color, this is a strong, full-bodied tea loved by some as a morning pick-me-up.

Ceylon: Grown in Sri Lanka, this tea is often labeled "high grown" because it is cultivated at an altitude of 4,000 feet (1,219 m). Mostly used in blends, this is a strong, rich, full-bodied tea of light golden color.

China Black: A blend of tea from Keemun and the China mainland. A mellow tea with a distinctive smoky taste.

Darjeeling: Known as the "champagne of teas," it is grown in the Himalayan foothills and is available only three to four weeks a year. A very expensive tea, mostly used in blends. Famous for its fruity bouquet and light, full-bodied taste.

Earl Grey: A blend of Chinese and Indian black teas scented with oil of bergamot, a citrus fruit. An incredibly fragrant, full-bodied tea.

English Breakfast: A blend of Ceylon and Indian teas. A full-bodied "typical" English brew, popular as a breakfast tea.

Irish Breakfast: A blend of Assam and Ceylon teas. A strong, sharp brew, gives a "full cup of tea."

Keemun: The best of the China blacks, it is called the "burgundy of teas" by connoisseurs. Superior flavor with a wonderful flowery aroma.

Lapsang Souchong: A large-leaf black tea from the south of China. It has an unusual deep, rich, smoky aroma and flavor.

Prince of Wales: A blend of the finest Keemun teas. A robust tea with rich, golden color.

LAPSANG SOUCHONG/EARL GREY TEA

❋

This blend gives a wonderfully smoky, fragrant cup of tea. It is an old recipe that catches people by surprise with its rich fullness.

Follow the directions for a perfect cup of tea. The measurements for this brew are half and half: half a teaspoon of Earl Grey and half a teaspoon of Lapsang Souchong per cup. If you are using tea bags, you will have to make at least two cups to get the measurements right. We like to drink this tea with milk; sugar seems superfluous. Serve hot.

OOLONG TEAS

China Oolong: A partially fermented tea. A light brew with a lovely fragrance.

Formosa Oolong: Native to Indochina, this tea is only available five weeks a year. An amber-colored broth, delicate in taste, and considered to be the best of the oolongs.

Mainland Oolong: A delicate Chinese tea with a beautiful aroma, sometimes scented with flowers.

GREEN TEAS

Gunpowder: A grade of tea in which the leaves are rolled into small pellets. Produces a clear, aromatic brew, which can sometimes be bitter.

Hyson: A "pan-fried" tea. A clear, light, gentle brew that leans toward being sharp or bitter.

Orange pekoe (pronounced peck-ō, and meaning "white hair"), is a grade of tea, referring to the size of the leaf. Orange pekoe is used in blends to give life or body to the infusion. The flavor varies with the place of origin or the processing involved. It is thought that at one time it was flavored with orange—hence its name, orange pekoe.

With the ever-increasing popularity of tea, three variations of traditional tea have come into vogue:

Specialty Teas The Chinese flavored their teas centuries ago. Specialty teas have black tea for a base and are flavored with spices, fruit, or other ingredients such as almond, cinnamon, lemon, or mint. These teas are distinguished from herbal teas by the fact that they contain caffeine. Specialty teas are finding increasing favor as morning or after-dinner drinks, particularly the fruit teas. These are refreshing, clear the palate, and are wonderful as dessert teas. Made with distilled essences of the fruit and/or fruit oils, these teas are available in a large variety of flavors.

For the best brew, it is best to buy fruit teas rather than try to make them yourself, since the process involved in creating your own fruit teas is not easy. Simply adding a concentrate or fruit juice does not achieve the desired effect and it will dilute the flavor of the tea. However, there are two possible alternatives to making fruit teas:

❁ Put a spoonful of fruit preserves in your cup before adding the tea. Bear in mind that doing this will sweeten the tea.

❁ Put a slice of lemon or orange rind (a two-by-one-quarter-inch slice per cup) in the teapot with the tea leaves. Pour in boiling water and

let the mixture steep for five minutes. The boiling water will release the fruit oil, thereby lightly flavoring the tea.

Decaffeinated Teas Tea contains less caffeine than coffee; coffee has one and a half grains of caffeine per cup, tea has less than one grain. Nevertheless, many people have decided to eliminate caffeine from their diets entirely. In recognition of this, most tea companies are producing decaffeinated teas.

Today, most tea manufacturers no longer decaffeinate their teas through a chemical process—they use sparkling water instead. Those who use this process let you know, so read the box labels.

Decaffeinated teas are also being produced by not using tea at all. Rather, a compilation of herbs that simulate the taste of tea are substituted. A word of caution. If the box lists "maté" in its ingredients, the tea has caffeine —maté is a South American caffeine plant. Herbal teas do not use black teas and are naturally caffeine-free.

Herbal Teas To the purist, herbal teas are not really tea at all. They are considered to be infusions, or in Europe, tisanes. An herbal tea is made from a combination of herbs, leaves, flowers, plants, berries, and spices. They are naturally caffeine-free, provide a wonderful alternative to caffeinated drinks and carbonated sodas, and are good both hot and cold.

Traditionally used as "medicines," herbal teas can act as mild digestives, help lift depression, soothe you to sleep, and slenderize the physique. The myriad benefits of herbal teas also carry with them an element of caution. Exercise care in the amounts and kinds of herbal tea you drink. In the interest of safety, you should limit your intake to two or three cups per day, moderation being the key. Not all herbal teas are safe to drink as a beverage. Read labels. If you prepare your own mixes, use only those herbs that are beverage-safe.

BEVERAGE-SAFE HERBS

❖

Listed below are those ingredients safe to drink as a beverage. We suggest seeking expert advice before using herbs and plants not listed.

Alfalfa	Lemongrass
Catnip	Linden flower
Chamomile	Nettle
Chicory root	Peppermint
Elder flowers	Rosehip
Fennel	Red and Black raspberry
Fenugreek	Red clover
Ginger	Spearmint
Goldenrod	Slippery elm bark
Hibiscus	Yarrow

TEA RECIPES

A Perfect Pot of Tea

The round shape of the teapot was designed by the Chinese, who used a musk melon as the model.

To brew a perfect pot of tea, boil fresh, cold tap water in a kettle. (Cold water is essential because it has a greater oxygen content and gives the tea a fuller flavor.) While the water is boiling, warm the teapot with hot water. Once the teapot is warmed, pour out the water and put in the tea. Use one teaspoon of leaves or one tea bag per cup of tea. Some people like to add one extra for the pot. Once the water is boiling, bring the teapot over to it and pour it in the teapot immediately. Boiling water drops in temperature the moment you lift it from the flame, so by bringing the teapot to the kettle rather than vice versa, you have the hottest water possible. Let the tea brew three to five minutes. For reliability in flavor, always "brew by the clock, not the color." Serve hot.

A Perfect Cup of Tea

Tea bags were invented by Mr. Thomas Sullivan of New York City. Sullivan was a coffee and tea merchant who wanted to send samples of his tea to customers in the hope of generating sales, so in 1904, he had little white silk bags made up and filled them with tea. To his surprise, orders for tea poured in, but they wanted it delivered in the bags. Ladies had found they could make a wonderful cup of tea by pouring boiling water through the bags.

To make a perfect cup of tea, you need the following:

1 tea bag
1 cup
Boiling water

Place the tea bag in a cup. A 10-ounce cup is best, but lesser amounts, such as an 8-ounce cup, work fine. Heat cold, fresh tap water in a kettle until it boils.

Bring the cup over to the kettle and pour boiling water over the tea bag, leaving enough room in the cup to accommodate milk or lemon. Dunk the tea bag once or twice. Let the tea brew for 3 to 5 minutes. As a tea bag can hold up to 7 times its weight in water, squeeze the bag as you remove it from the cup. Serve hot.

Iced Tea

MAKES 8 12-OUNCE GLASSES
(WITH ICE).

Of the 45 billion cups of tea consumed each year in the United States, 37 billion are sipped in the form of iced tea. Iced tea was invented in 1904 at the St. Louis World Fair by an English tea merchant who was there to introduce Americans to Eastern teas. It was a hot day and fairgoers bypassed his pavilion for those who served cold drinks. In desperation, he poured his tea into ice-filled glasses. It was an instant hit, and has remained so.

2   quarts cold, fresh tap water
12   tea bags (your choice)

The rule of thumb when making iced tea is to use 50 percent more tea than when making hot tea. This amount of tea gives you a flavor that is not diluted despite melting ice. Pour 1 quart of water into a saucepan and 1 quart of water into a 2-quart pitcher. Heat the water in the pan until boiling. Remove the pan from the heat, add the tea bags to the pan, and let sit for 10 minutes.

Remove the bags from the pan and pour the tea concentrate into the pitcher of cold water. Cover and refrigerate until cold, approximately 2 to 3 hours.

Because of tea solids, tea made this way sometimes becomes cloudy. The flavor isn't affected, but if this bothers you, pour a small amount of boiling water into the tea. This should clear it up.

SUN-BREWED ICED TEA

MAKES 4 12-OUNCE GLASSES
(WITH ICE).

1   quart cold, fresh tap water
6   tea bags (your choice)

Place the cold water in a glass container. Put the tea bags into the water. Cover and set out in the sun for 2 hours.

Serve over ice or refrigerate until ready to use.

MINT TEA JULEPS

MAKES 4 12-OUNCE GLASSES.

6   tablespoons sugar
6   tablespoons water
12 large mint leaves,
      approximately (depending
      on your personal taste)
Sun-Brewed Iced Tea, chilled
4   straws

Put the sugar and the water in a small pan and bring to a boil. Continue to boil for 2 minutes. Remove from the heat and cool to room temperature.

Fill 4 12-ounce glasses halfway with ice. Tear mint leaves with your fingers and put them over the ice (3 leaves per glass). Spoon 2 tablespoons of sugar into each glass.

Pour iced tea into the glass, filling it. Stir. Place a straw in each glass. Serve.

LEMONADE TEA

MAKES 4 12-OUNCE GLASSES.

2   cups lemonade, approximately
1   quart cold, fresh tap water
4   tea bags (your choice)
2   lemon tea bags

Fill ice cube trays with the lemonade. You will want approximately 6 ice cubes per glass of tea, so adjust the lemonade measurement as necessary. Freeze until the lemonade cubes are hard.

Meanwhile, put the cold water in a glass container and add the tea bags. Place the container in the sun and let brew for approximately 2 to 3 hours. When the tea is brewed let it chill in the refrigerator for at least 1 hour.

Fill a 12-ounce glass with lemonade cubes, then pour the chilled tea over the cubes until you have a full glass. Serve.

You can make up the cubes several days in advance and store them in plastic bags in the freezer. The tea can be made the day before and stored, covered, in the refrigerator.

Sun Brewed Iced Tea: cold and refreshing on a summer's day.

CHAPTER TWO

HOUSE SPECIALTEAS

Clove-Studded Lemon Wedges

Welsh Currant Cookies

Clotted Cream

Alice Paradis' Peach Preserves

Strawberry Jam

Fruit Butters

Serves 6.

AT SPECIALTEAS, WHENEVER WE PLAN A TEA FOR A client, there is always an in-depth discussion of the food preferences of both the client and their guests. This is important, for the primary rule of thumb at a Tea is for everyone to derive great satisfaction from the meal before them. The meal should be well prepared, appealing to the eyes, and pleasing to the palate. Keeping this in mind, there are preparation practices we always adhere to:

❀ Use fresh, thinly sliced bread. Normal slices of bread change the taste of the sandwich because it increases the ratio of bread to filling, and you cannot achieve the delicate look or taste that Tea sandwiches have.

❀ Every slice of bread used for a sandwich should be covered with a very thin coating of butter. This stops the filling from leaking through, thus preventing the bread from becoming soggy. Use real butter, not margarine or a mixture of butter and margarine. Butter adds a richness and substance to each sandwich that is evocative of Tea as a whole.

❀ Plan on a total of two whole sandwiches or eight sandwich pieces per person. It sounds like a lot, but the bread is thin and once the crusts are cut off, the size of the sandwich is greatly diminished. Guests tend to approach Tea sandwiches with a healthy appetite. Because they are so small, most people aren't really aware of how many they are eating. If there are some left over, have a small Tea for yourself the next day. They will keep.

❀ We generally cut each tea sandwich in one of three ways:

—into four small squares, achieved by cutting two intersecting lines (as in the shape of a cross) in the sandwich;

—into three parallel pieces, achieved by three lengthwise cuts in the sandwich, making sure the pieces are of equal size. In England toast is often cut in this manner to eat with boiled eggs and the pieces are called egg soldiers;

—the exception to the above would be to cut your sandwiches into different shapes, such as stars and hearts, by using cookie cutters. Depending on the size of the cutters, you will have to adjust the number of sandwiches you need to make to fulfill your serving requirements. The disadvantage to cutting your sandwiches this way is that there will be a certain amount of waste of both filling and bread.

❀ Always serve cucumber sandwiches. They are refreshing and cut through the richness of the other foods. This is not reflected in the menus; however, two different recipes for cucumber sandwiches are provided if you choose to follow our custom.

❀ Always serve jam and clotted cream with the scones. This is only a suggestion, however, because some people prefer to keep things simple and have their scones plain or with butter.

❈ Because people have a tendency to eat so many sandwiches, their appetites lose their edge when it is time for the scones. For this reason we keep the scones small. Large scones are simply too much for people to eat once they are covered with jam and cream. In this case less is absolutely best.

Ceylon tea served with slices of pound cake.

❈ What applies to scones also applies to pastries. If you are making individual tarts and cakes, keep them small.

It has been our experience that people generally know what to expect at a Tea. They are familiar with the basics. What they don't know and want to see are the extras. What additional treats will there be? What kind of jam? Will there be clove-studded lemons? We think these little frills are important. At any Tea we serve, we make sure the following are available:

- ❈ clove-studded lemon slices
- ❈ Welsh currant cookies
- ❈ clotted cream
- ❈ a choice of two of the following:
- —homemade peach preserves
- —strawberry jam
- —fruit butters

These small touches add the finish to your Tea—they are the *"je ne sais quoi"* of the tea table.

Russian tea, to be served with cherry preserves, lemon and sugar, and Tea Cakes.

Tea break!

SERVING THE TEA

In the following chapters are recipes for tea and food. Before you read them it would be helpful for you to know a few of the Tea "procedures." Then, as you read the recipes and plan your Tea, it will be easier to create a mental picture of how it all will come together.

The first thing to do is to make two decisions: Are you serving brewed tea or using tea bags, and, is your Tea going to be served buffet-style or is it to be a "seated" Tea?

TEA BASICS

Plan on serving two to three cups of tea per person. Each person should have a cup, a saucer (if necessary), and a spoon. Since people take their tea in one of six ways— plain (often called black), with milk, with sugar, with milk and sugar, with lemon, and with lemon and sugar—make sure you have all of these accompaniments on hand. The sugar can either be cubes or granulated, although cubes are less messy. If you have tongs for the cubes, even better. The lemon should be set on a plate with a small fork. Some people serve lemon with tea by putting it in the cup and pouring the tea over it, but we prefer to place the lemon on the side (on the saucer) and let the guest add it. As an extra treat, we stud some of our lemons with cloves (see recipe, page 26) for added taste and fragrance.

BREWED TEA

If you are serving brewed tea, use a large enough teapot (two if necessary) so that all your guests are accommodated in a single pouring. As they are drinking the first cup, replenish the pots. It is wise to have help: one person to be the pourer and another to keep the kettle boiling, replenish the brew, and bring in the food. You can do all of this yourself, but you may decide you don't want to keep leaving your guests. Enlist a friend to help or hire someone for a few hours.

When the teapot is not in use, cover it with a tea cozy to keep it hot. If you don't have a cozy, an attractive tea towel, folded and placed over the spout and lid, will help. Keeping the tea hot is not as much of a problem with a silver service, since the metal retains the heat.

When you serve brewed tea you need an attractive strainer to prevent the leaves from going into the cup. Place the strainer in a small bowl by the pourer. Place the strainer on top of each cup before the tea is poured, then remove it and put back in the bowl. Excess leaves can be tipped into the bowl to prevent the strainer from clogging. The pourer then asks each guest what they would like in their tea, adds whatever is desired, and hands the cup to the guest. This continues until each guest is served. This is the standard method for a seated Tea. If you are having a buffet-style Tea, you may still want to have a pourer or you may choose to let the guests serve themselves.

As said before, always keep a kettle—or two—boiling while the party is in full swing, thereby insuring that fresh, hot pots of tea are no problem. Simply dump out the used leaves, put in fresh leaves, and pour in the water. A friend of ours bypasses the need for using a tea strainer by brewing her tea with a Melita-type drip coffee maker. The measurements are the same as those used for a regular pot of tea. She puts the tea in a paper filter and pours the water over the leaves, letting it drip down into the container. A low flame keeps the tea hot until the dripping process is finished. The tea is then transferred to the serving pot. This method produces a good cup of tea and eliminates some of the fuss.

The key to having a Tea is to be organized and prepared. Make sure everything is set up beforehand and it will be very easy to keep the pots filled and the flow of the party going.

From the Thanksgiving Tea: Red Cabbage and Bacon Vinaigrette Tarts served with Assam tea.

TEA BAGS

If you choose to use tea bags, make sure you have enough for each guest to use a fresh bag for each cup of tea. Arrange the tea bags on a small platter or in a bowl. Using tea bags gives you the opportunity to provide your guests with an assortment of teas from which to choose. Place the hot water in an attractive urn or china pot that can be refilled as necessary.

TEA FOOD

The food you serve at a Tea is the same whether it is served buffet-style or seated. You will need a fork, knife, plate, and napkin for each guest. If you serve buffet-style, set the food out on a table and let the guests help themselves. We always put the jams and clotted cream in bowls with spoons, which facilitates putting these toppings on the scones.

SERVING THE FOOD

There is a correct order in which the food should be eaten. First the sandwiches, followed by the scones (which are lovely cut in half, spread with jam, and topped with a dollop of clotted cream, or vice versa), and lastly the sweets, with cups of tea offered throughout. A buffet offers guests more freedom of choice, so don't be surprised if some disregard this prescribed order.

When you serve people who are seated, the Tea foods should be served in the order mentioned above. The jams and cream should be placed on the table and left there throughout the meal. The food is brought to the guests on platters or trays and passed by the hostess or server. Make sure each guest has had their fill of a course before passing the next one. Cookies and small cakes can be placed on the table, allowing the guests to help themselves while the hostess or server passes around the larger desserts.

The important thing to remember in all of this is that you and your guests should enjoy the occasion. Do not be frightened by the ceremony; relax and let the party flow. The more Teas you give, the more effortless they will become. You do not have to follow anyone's rules: make your own, create your own traditions. Simply remember to have fun making the food, serving your guests, and collecting compliments.

The following recipes are the little extras that can be served at any tea. Finally, since it is your Tea, it is important to remember that what we are giving you are the guidelines; it is for you to decide what suits you and your guests best. It may mean you choose to pull a Tea together from several different menus, serve less of one sandwich and more of another, or none at all. Do whatever you choose to insure that both you and your guests are delighted with your special Tea.

Filled Chinese Pancakes.

Clove-Studded Lemon Wedges

MAKES 8 WEDGES.

1 medium-size lemon
Whole cloves
Toothpicks

Early in the day of your Tea, wash a lemon under warm water with a vegetable brush. Dry the lemon thoroughly.

Using a sharp paring knife, draw 8 equally spaced lines from the top of the lemon to the bottom. Going down the length of these lines, puncture continuous holes with a toothpick. Push a whole clove into each of these holes until you have 8 complete lines. Place the lemon aside until Tea time.

While you are boiling the water for the tea, cut the wedges by centering a knife between 2 rows of cloves and slicing. Continue until you have cut out all 8 wedges.

Welsh Currant Cookies

MAKES APPROXIMATELY 6 1/2 DOZEN COOKIES.

4 cups flour
1 3/4 cups sugar
4 teaspoons baking powder
1 teaspoon cinnamon
1/4 teaspoon nutmeg
1 cup shortening (such as Crisco)
1 cup milk, approximately
1 10-ounce package currants

Mix the dry ingredients together in a bowl. Cut in shortening. Pour in milk, a little at a time, mixing to make a firm dough. If necessary, add more milk (up to 1 cup), being careful that you don't end up with a sticky dough. Add the currants.

Roll out the dough on a floured surface to 1/4-inch thickness. Cut out the cookies with a 2-inch biscuit cutter or glass.

Over low heat, cook the cookies on an ungreased griddle or skillet until very brown, about 2 minutes per side. Cool and serve. The cookies can be frozen.

Clotted Cream

MAKES 1 1/3 CUPS; SERVES 4 TO 6.

THE CREAM USED IN ENGLAND IS NOT available here, although there are a number of substitutes and facsimiles available. We use the following:

1 cup heavy cream, at room temperature
1/3 cup sour cream, at room temperature
1 tablespoon confectioner's sugar

One hour before serving, pour the heavy cream into a bowl and whip until soft peaks form. Whisk in the sour cream and sugar, continuing to beat until the mixture is very thick.

Place in the refrigerator and chill until it is time to serve.

If you want to make this ahead of time, it should last 4 to 6 hours in the refrigerator.

ALICE PARADIS' PEACH PRESERVES

MAKES 4 PINTS.

2 quarts peaches
(approximately 6 to 8
peaches per quart,
depending on the size)
1/4 cup lemon juice
7 cups sugar
1 teaspoon cinnamon

Peel and pit the peaches. Place in a large saucepan and sprinkle with lemon juice (this protects the peaches from browning). Mix in the sugar. Cover the pan and let stand overnight.

The next day, bring the mixture to a boil over medium-high heat. Once the mixture has boiled, turn the heat down to low and simmer slowly until the syrup thickens and the peaches are clear. Add the cinnamon, stirring well. Skim any bubbles off the top, making sure all the foam is removed.

After skimming, crush the peaches in the saucepan using a potato masher.

Pour the peaches into 4 hot, sterilized pint-size mason jars. Fill to 1/2 inch from the top. Wipe the tops of the jars with a clean, damp cloth. Screw the lids on tightly. Turn the jars upside down, allowing the lids to heat and seal.

After the jars have cooled, return to the upright position and let sit for at least 24 hours. Label and date.

Store in a cool, dry place. The jam will have a shelf life of approximately 1 year.

STRAWBERRY JAM

MAKES 8 HALF PINTS.

9 cups fresh strawberries
2 tablespoons lemon juice
8 cups sugar

Wash, dry, hull, and halve the strawberries. Put them with the lemon juice in a large pot. Heat over medium heat until the mixture begins to simmer. Cook at a simmer until the fruit becomes soft, approximately 15 minutes.

Add the sugar, stirring until dissolved. Raise the heat to high and bring the mixture to a boil. Continue cooking for 30 minutes or until thick. Remove from heat, skim off any foam, and let sit for 5 minutes.

Pour the jam into hot, sterilized mason jars. Fill to 1/2 inch from the top. Wipe the tops of the jars with a clean, damp cloth. Screw the lids on tightly. Turn the jars upside down, allowing the lids to heat and seal.

After the jars have cooled, return to the upright position and let sit for at least 24 hours before using. Label and date the jars. Store in a cool, dry place.

The jam will have a shelf life of approximately 1 year. Should you open a jar and find any sign of mold or encounter a peculiar odor, discard it immediately.

FRUIT BUTTERS

MAKES APPROXIMATELY 1 1/2 CUPS.

1/2 pound butter, at room
temperature
1/2 cup of your favorite fruit
preserve

Place the butter and preserves in a bowl. Using a mixer, a food processor fitted with the metal blade, or a blender, whip the 2 ingredients together until well blended.

Spoon the butter into a serving dish or ramekin. Chill until ready to serve.

CHAPTER THREE

A BRITISH CREAM TEA

Smoked Salmon and Dill Sandwiches

Curried Egg-Mayonnaise Sandwiches

Cucumber Sandwiches

Roquefort, Walnut, and Cognac Sandwiches

Currant Scones

Scottish Petticoat Tails

Fruit Tarts

Classic Sponge Cake

Prince of Wales Tea (or your choice)

Serves 6.

WHEN ANNA, THE SEVENTH DUCHESS OF BEDFORD, MADE HER FIRST eloquent request for afternoon refreshment, she started a tradition that is still beloved a century and a half later. The British Cream Tea is the epitome of this afternoon pleasure. A Cream Tea is so called because it is just that, a Tea with clotted cream and the products of milk: butter, whipped cream, and custards. These, and a wonderful array of sandwiches, scones, cookies, cakes, and pastries, grace the tea table. The combinations are endless.

Mind you, the British do not indulge in a Cream Tea every afternoon; it is as much an occasion for them as it is for us. Their daily Teas are considerably pared down. They may be as simple as tea and toast, crumpets heated over the fire, or slices of a simple cake.

But when the British do a Cream Tea, it's heaven. There simply is no comparison, as we found to our delight. Their Teas are remarkable not only in the choices available but for the freshness and wonderful quality of the foods they serve: the swirling richness of the cream, the buttery crispness of shortbread, and the melting appeal of cakes that are both substantive and light. We have tried to remain faithful to the memories of these Teas by choosing those foods that are classics.

SMOKED SALMON AND DILL SANDWICHES

MAKES 12 PIECES.

6 thin slices wheat bread
Unsalted butter
3 ounces smoked salmon, sliced
1 teaspoon chopped fresh dill

Spread each slice of bread with a thin coating of butter. Divide the smoked salmon evenly between 3 slices of bread. Sprinkle $1/3$ teaspoon of fresh dill over each sandwich. Cover the sandwiches with the remaining bread slices. Trim the crusts. Cut each sandwich into 4 pieces.

CURRIED EGG-MAYONNAISE SANDWICHES

MAKES 12 PIECES.

4 thin slices white bread
4 thin slices wheat bread
Unsalted butter
Curried Egg Salad

Spread each slice of bread with a thin coating of butter. Divide the Curried Egg Salad between the 4 slices of white bread and spread evenly. Top the white bread with the wheat bread. Trim the crusts. Cut the sandwiches into 3 parallel pieces.

Curried Egg Salad

MAKES $3/4$ CUP.

2 hard-boiled eggs, peeled
$1/2$ cup mayonnaise
$1/2$ teaspoon curry powder

Finely chop the eggs. Mix in the mayonnaise and curry powder, making sure all the ingredients are combined.

This will keep in the refrigerator, well covered, for 3 days.

CUCUMBER SANDWICHES

MAKES 12 PIECES.

$1/2$ medium cucumber, peeled and thinly sliced
1 tablespoon apple cider vinegar
Unsalted butter
6 thin slices white bread
Salt (to taste)
Pepper (to taste)

Combine the cucumber and vinegar in a bowl. Toss to blend. Let sit for $1/2$ hour. Drain off excess liquid.

Spread a thin coating of butter on each slice of bread. On 3 slices of bread, place the cucumber slices, making sure the bread is well covered (you'll need 6 to 8 slices of cucumber). Salt and pepper each sandwich. Cover with the remaining slices of buttered bread. Trim the crusts. Cut each sandwich into 4 pieces.

Currant Scones with jam and clotted cream (see recipe on page 32).

ROQUEFORT, WALNUT, AND COGNAC SANDWICHES

MAKES 12 PIECES.

1/2 cup walnuts
1/4 pound Roquefort cheese, at
    room temperature
2 tablespoons cognac
6 thin slices white bread
Unsalted butter

Toast the walnuts under the broiler for approximately 8 to 10 minutes or until golden brown. Cool and finely chop.

While the walnuts are toasting, blend the cheese with the cognac.

Spread each slice of bread with a thin coating of butter.

Spoon the cheese mixture, dividing evenly, on 3 slices of bread and spread over each slice. Sprinkle a full tablespoon of nuts over the cheese. Top each sandwich with the remaining bread slices, pressing down firmly.

Trim the crusts. Cut each sandwich into 4 pieces.

CURRANT SCONES

MAKES APPROXIMATELY
10 TO 12 SCONES.

2 cups flour
1/4 cup sugar
2 teaspoons baking powder
1 teaspoon salt
3 tablespoons unsalted butter,
    cold
3/4 cup milk
1 egg
1/2 cup currants
1 egg yolk
2 tablespoons cold water

Preheat oven to 350° F.

Sift the dry ingredients together. Using a pastry blender or 2 knives, cut the butter into the dry ingredients until the mixture is crumbly.

Beat the milk and egg together. Pour into the dry ingredients and stir until well blended. Add the currants, stirring until well combined.

Prepare a flat surface by flouring it well (the dough will be slightly wet and will absorb the flour quickly). Place the dough on the flat surface. Knead briefly (once or twice) and pat the dough until it is 3/4 inch thick. Cut out the scones with a 2 1/2-inch biscuit cutter and place on a greased baking sheet.

Beat the egg yolk with the cold water. Using a pastry brush, glaze each scone with this mixture. Bake for 25 to 30 minutes or until golden brown. Serve hot or cold, with jam and clotted cream, if desired.

SCOTTISH PETTICOAT TAILS

MAKES 8 OR 16 WEDGES.

2 cups sifted all-purpose flour
1/2 teaspoon baking powder
1 cup unsalted butter
1/2 cup sugar
1 tablespoon grated lemon rind,
    optional

Preheat oven to 300° F.

Sift together the flour and baking powder. Put the butter in a food processor fitted with the metal blade and cream. Add sugar to the butter and process for 30 seconds or until well blended. Add the flour and baking powder, processing until a dough is formed. Do not overwork. Put in the lemon rind (if using) and pulse the processor until just blended in.

Remove the dough from the food processor and put it in a greased 9-inch pie plate. Pat the dough down with your fingers, distributing it evenly over the bottom of the pie plate.

With the back of a knife, carefully cut the dough into either 8 or 16 pie-shape wedges. Prick each wedge in several places with a fork. Bake for 30 minutes or until golden brown. Remove from oven. The wedges will run together while cooking, so retrace the original knife cuts while the shortbread is still hot. Let the cookies cool completely.

When cool, remove the first wedge carefully. The petticoat tails will stay fresh for a week if stored in an airtight container.

NOTE: If you choose not to use a food processor, just follow the instructions and mix by hand.

Prince of Wales Tea and Scottish Petticoat Tails garnished with orange and strawberry.

Fruit Tarts with lemon curd.

FRUIT TARTS

MAKES 6 TARTS.

Sweet Pastry

MAKES ENOUGH DOUGH
FOR 6 TARTS.

1 cup all-purpose flour
2 tablespoons sugar
¼ teaspoon salt
5½ tablespoons butter
1 egg, slightly beaten

Combine the flour, sugar, and salt in a food processor fitted with the metal blade and pulse 2 or 3 times. Process in butter until the dough is crumbly. Add enough of the egg, approximately one half, to form a dough. Wrap the dough in plastic wrap and chill for 1 hour.

Preheat oven to 350°F.

Roll out half of the dough on a lightly floured surface. Cut out 6 4-inch circles. (Freeze the remaining dough, well wrapped. It will last 3 months.)

Place a dough circle in each of 6 fluted tart pans, 3 inches in diameter and ½ inch high. Press down and around gently. Remove any excess. Gently prick the dough with a fork.

Bake in a preheated oven for 15 to 30 minutes or until starting to brown. Cool in the tins until ready to use.

Judie's Lemon Curd

MAKES 2 CUPS.

1¼ cups sugar
4 eggs
Juice of 4 lemons
(approximately ½ cup)
12 tablespoons unsalted butter
Grated rind of 2 lemons
(optional)
Fresh raspberries (for final step
of assembly)

Beat the sugar and eggs until light and fluffy. Blend in the lemon juice.

Pour the mixture into a saucepan and heat over a low flame until hot. Add the butter, 1 tablespoon at a time, until completely melted and blended. Raise the heat to medium and cook until thick. Stir well as it thickens to prevent sticking and burning. Fold in the rind, if desired. Cool.

To assemble the tarts, fill each shell with 2 tablespoons of Judie's Lemon Curd. Starting in the center and working outward, cover the top of the tarts with fresh raspberries, approximately 20 per tart. Refrigerate until ready to serve.

These tarts are best if made within 24 hours of serving.

CLASSIC SPONGE CAKE

MAKES 1 9-INCH LAYER CAKE.

2 eggs
²/₃ cup sugar
1 cup self-rising cake flour
4 tablespoons unsalted, melted,
  cooled butter
½ cup milk
1 teaspoon vanilla
1 cup damson plum preserves
  (or your favorite)
Confectioner's sugar

Preheat oven to 325°F.

Beat the eggs in a mixer on high speed until they are thick and lemon-colored, approximately 5 minutes. Gradually add the sugar, continuing to beat until the mixture is very thick and falls in thick folds when you lift the beaters from the batter. Add the flour, beating just until well blended. Combine the butter, milk, and vanilla. Add to batter. Mix until well combined. Do not overbeat.

Pour batter into a greased 9-inch cake pan. Place in the preheated oven and bake for 25 to 30 minutes or until golden brown and a toothpick inserted in the center comes out clean.

Let cool in the pan for 10 minutes, then turn the cake out onto a cake rack and cool completely. When cake is cool, slice into 2 even layers. Gently spread the preserves evenly over the bottom layer. Replace the top of the cake. Dust the top with confectioner's sugar.

This cake tastes best when made and eaten the same day.

Classic sponge cake filled with preserves.

CHAPTER FOUR

AN AMERICAN CREAM TEA

Roast Beef Sandwiches with Horseradish Sauce

Waldorf Chicken Salad Sandwiches

Goat Cheese and Sun-dried Tomato Tartlets

Curried Tuna Salad Sandwiches

Walnut Scones

Ginger Snaps

Tangy Lemon Bundt Cake

Vanilla Custard Fruit Tarts

Ceylon Tea (or your choice)

Serves 6.

ON DECEMBER 16, 1773, WHEN THE COLONISTS DUMPED TEA OVERBOARD at that famous tea party in Boston, they were revolting against the taxes that came with the beverage, not against the tea. This act led to a deep schism between the American colonists and Britain. It didn't actually stop people from drinking tea; it just stopped them from having tea with the Brits. Two hundred years later, this, of course, has changed. The wounds have healed and the two countries now refer to each other as cousins. The bonds between the two countries are so firmly established that their cultures often overlap.

Of the many wonderful gifts the British have given us, Afternoon Tea is clearly a favorite. Americans often call this meal "High Tea," pointing out the aura of majesty and mystery with which Americans view Tea. (High Tea is something else entirely that we will explain in a later chapter.)

An American Cream Tea can be very simple. Following the British example—for we consider its basic design and variations perfect—it is easy to convert this custom to American tastes. We stick to the structure of a three-course meal. Our variations come in the food choices we make, borrowed from the myriad of cultures that flourish in North America, and from American classics such as Thanksgiving.

ROAST BEEF SANDWICHES WITH HORSERADISH SAUCE

MAKES 16 PIECES.

2 tablespoons mayonnaise
1 tablespoon prepared horseradish
8 thin slices white bread
Unsalted butter
4 ounces thinly sliced roast beef
Salt (to taste)
Pepper (to taste)

Combine the mayonnaise and horseradish in a small bowl. Set aside.

Spread each slice of bread with a thin coating of butter.

Put 1 ounce of roast beef on each of 4 slices of bread, folding it to conform to the size of the bread. Season with salt and pepper. Spoon a teaspoon of the horseradish sauce over the beef on each sandwich.

If you would like a sharper taste, use 1½ teaspoons of the sauce. Top the sandwiches with the remaining bread slices. Trim the crusts. Cut each sandwich into 4 pieces.

WALDORF CHICKEN SALAD SANDWICHES

MAKES 12 PIECES.

Salad
3 cups cooked chicken, medium diced
¾ cup walnuts, coarsely chopped
¾ cup Granny Smith apples, small diced
½ cup golden raisins
½ cup celery, small diced
2 scallions, finely sliced
Salt (to taste)
Pepper (to taste)

Dressing
1 cup mayonnaise
½ cup sour cream
¼ cup cider vinegar
1 tablespoon honey
6 thin slices whole wheat bread

Butter

Place the salad ingredients in a large bowl, tossing to combine.

In a smaller bowl, whisk the dressing ingredients together. Pour the dressing over the salad and mix well. Season with salt and pepper. Chill about 2 hours.

To assemble the sandwiches, spread the bread with a thin coating of butter.

Spread 2 to 3 tablespoons Waldorf Chicken Salad on each of the 3 slices of bread. Top the sandwiches with the remaining bread. Trim the crusts. Cut each sandwich into 4 pieces.

Goat Cheese and Sun-Dried Tomato Tartlets

MAKES 8 TARTLETS.

Tartlet Shells

MAKES 8 SHELLS.

8   thin slices white bread
2¹/₂   tablespoons melted butter

Preheat oven to 350°F.

Cut 1 circle out of each slice of bread with a 3-inch round biscuit cutter, preferably with crimped edges. Lightly brush melted butter on both sides of each round. Press each round into a cup in a cupcake tin. The edges of the bread rounds will come up the cup sides slightly. Bake for 10 to 15 minutes. Watch the shells closely, as you want them golden brown. They have a tendency to become too dark.

These shells can be stored up to a week in an airtight container.

Goat Cheese and Sun-Dried Tomato Spread

MAKES ¹/₃ CUP.

¹/₄   cup goat cheese, at room
      temperature
2   tablespoons heavy cream
    (milk can be substituted)
2   tablespoons minced sun-dried
    tomatoes
2   sun-dried tomatoes, each cut
    into 8 thin slices

Goat Cheese and Sun-Dried Tomato Tartlets served with Roast Beef and Waldorf Chicken Salad Sandwiches.

Combine the goat cheese and heavy cream until smooth. Add the minced sun-dried tomatoes, mixing thoroughly. This spread can be kept in the refrigerator, covered, for 3 days.

To assemble the tartlets, fill each shell with the goat cheese and sun-dried tomato spread, dividing it evenly between the 8 shells. On top of each shell crisscross 2 slices of sun-dried tomatoes.

Curried Tuna Salad Sandwiches

MAKES 12 PIECES.

1 3¹/₄-ounce can solid white
   tuna, drained
1 tablespoon finely sliced
   scallion
3 tablespoons currants
3 tablespoons finely chopped
   walnuts
¹/₂ cup mayonnaise
1¹/₂ teaspoons curry powder
3 thin slices white bread
3 thin slices wheat bread

Butter

Put the tuna in a small bowl, flaking with a fork to separate the meat. Add the rest of the ingredients and mix well. You can use for sandwiches immediately. Making it the day before allows time for the flavors to meld. This salad will stay in a refrigerator for a maximum of 3 days.

To assemble the sandwiches, spread 3 thin slices of white bread and 3 thin slices of wheat bread with a coating of butter.

Divide the Curried Tuna Salad between the 3 slices of white bread, spreading it evenly. Cover each sandwich with the wheat bread slices.

Trim the crusts. Cut each sandwich into 4 pieces.

Walnut Scones and tea.

Walnut Scones

MAKES APPROXIMATELY 10 SCONES.

2 cups flour
¹/₄ cup sugar
2 teaspoons baking powder
1 teaspoon salt
3 tablespoons unsalted butter,
   cold
³/₄ cup milk
1 egg
¹/₂ cup walnuts, coarsely
   chopped
1 egg yolk
2 tablespoons cold water

Preheat oven to 350°F.

Sift the dry ingredients together. Using a pastry blender or 2 knives, cut the butter into the dry ingredients until crumbly. Beat the milk and egg together. Pour into the dry ingredients, stirring until a dough is formed. Add the chopped walnuts, combining well. Using an ice cream scoop, form the scones and place on a greased baking sheet.

Beat the egg yolk with the cold water. Using a pastry brush, glaze each scone with this mixture. Bake for 25 to 30 minutes or until golden brown.

Serve hot or cold with jam and clotted cream, if desired.

GINGER SNAPS

MAKES APPROXIMATELY
4 DOZEN COOKIES.

This is a 100-year-old recipe.

1 cup molasses
1/3 cup shortening (such as
     Crisco)
3/4 teaspoon baking soda
1 teaspoon dry ginger
1/4 teaspoon salt
2 3/4 cups flour, approximately
Sugar

Preheat oven to 350°F.

Pour the molasses into a medium-size saucepan and bring to a boil.

Add the shortening, baking soda, ginger, and salt to the pan and stir well. When shortening has melted, turn off burner. When the mixture has cooled slightly, add enough flour so that the dough comes away from the sides of the pan. The dough is very elastic and will not require much flour.

Place the dough on a lightly floured surface and roll out very thin. Cut dough with a 2 1/2-inch round cookie cutter and place on a greased cookie sheet. Sprinkle each cookie lightly with sugar.

Bake until the cookies are firm and start to brown, approximately 10 minutes. You will be able to smell these cookies very strongly as they get done.

Cool on a rack.

Stored in an airtight container, these cookies will last up to 2 weeks.

TANGY LEMON BUNDT CAKE

MAKES 1 10-INCH BUNDT CAKE.

3 cups self-rising cake flour
2 1/2 cups sugar
4 large eggs, at room
     temperature
1/2 cup milk, at room temperature
1 tablespoon vanilla
3 1/2 sticks unsalted butter, at room
     temperature
1 1/2 tablespoons grated lemon peel
2/3 cup fresh lemon juice

Preheat oven to 350°F.

Sift together flour and 1 1/2 cups of the sugar. Beat eggs, milk, and vanilla together. Cut butter into pieces and add to dry ingredients along with 1/3 of the egg and milk mixture. Beat on medium until smooth, about 3 minutes. Add another third of the egg and milk, beating just until blended. Pour in remaining egg and milk and lemon peel. Mix just until blended. Pour into a 10-inch greased cake pan and press down with a spoon to push out air pockets. Bake 45 minutes to 1 hour, or until cake is golden brown and a toothpick inserted in the cake comes out clean.

Shortly before the cake is done, combine the lemon juice and remaining sugar in a small saucepan over high heat and cook until the sugar is dissolved. Lower the heat and cook for 2 minutes.

When the cake is done, remove from the oven and place on a cake rack. Spoon 1/2 cup of the glaze over the exposed part of the cake (this is actually the bottom of

the bundt) and let it sit for 10 minutes. Remove from rack. Coat a piece of wax paper with a light layer of cooking spray and place on the cake rack. Turn the cake onto the wax paper. Using a pastry brush, cover the top and sides of the cake with the rest of the glaze. Cool thoroughly. Remove cake to a platter and serve.

Wrapped well and refrigerated, this cake will last for at least 3 days. It can be frozen but must be well wrapped.

VANILLA CUSTARD FRUIT TARTS

MAKES 6 TARTS.

Follow the procedure for Fruit Tarts in the British Cream Tea (page 41), substituting this recipe for Judie's Lemon Curd.

1/2 cup sugar
4 tablespoons all-purpose flour
1/4 teaspoon salt
1 1/2 cups milk
2 egg yolks, beaten
2 teaspoons vanilla
1 tablespoon unsalted butter

Combine sugar, flour, and salt in a medium-size saucepan. Mix together the milk, egg yolks, and vanilla. Whisk the milk mixture into the flour mixture. Cook over low heat, stirring constantly, until the custard starts to thicken, about 5 minutes. Add the butter. Let the custard cook until very thick, 2 minutes. Remove from the heat and cool to room temperature. Fill the pastry shells with the custard.

CHAPTER FIVE

A SOUTHERN TEA

Fried Chicken 'n' Biscuit Sandwiches

Cajun Shrimp Sandwiches

Potato Salad in Cucumber Compotes

Ham Salad in Corn Muffin Cups

Coconut Cake

Pecan Scones

Sour Cream Sugar Cookies

Sun-Brewed Iced Tea

Serves 6.

THE AMERICAN SOUTH HAS ALWAYS EVOKED THOUGHTS OF GRACIOUSNESS and gentility. It is easy to conjure up images of ladies in large hats and white gloves sitting on the veranda having Tea. One senses balmy days and fragrant breezes floating about them as they sip delicately and eat sandwiches. It seems dreamlike.

The cuisine of the South consists of substantive foods that have become national favorites. Light, flaky biscuits (which are, by the way, first cousins to scones), tender, juicy fried chicken, and tall, moist cakes.

The Southern diet is one that has evolved over two centuries. It never strays very far from its origins, for Southerners are loyal people and these foods have always suited them and their way of life.

It suits us well, too. We've designed our Southern Tea to include all of our favorites. Nothing is nicer on a summer day than fried chicken and potato salad. We've changed the form but the essentials are there.

Everything can be prepared in advance, including the tea. Set out your Tea and as your guests begin to serve themselves, sit back and relax with a tall glass of iced tea.

As a change from iced tea, try a cup of Coronation tea.

FRIED CHICKEN 'N' BISCUIT SANDWICHES

MAKES 12 SANDWICHES.

Renny White's Biscuits

MAKES 1½ TO 2 DOZEN BISCUITS.

2½ cups sifted all-purpose flour
5 teaspoons baking powder
2 tablespoons sugar
1 teaspoon salt
5 tablespoons unsalted butter or shortening, cold
1 cup milk
2 tablespoons melted unsalted butter

Preheat oven to 425°F.

In a medium-size bowl, combine flour, baking powder, sugar, and salt. Using a pastry blender or 2 knives, cut in the shortening until the mixture is crumbly.

Pour in the milk and mix until a dough is formed. Place the dough on a lightly floured surface and pat it out until it is ½ inch thick.

Cut out the biscuits using a 2-inch biscuit cutter and place them on a greased baking sheet. Lightly brush the top of the biscuits with melted butter. Using a pastry brush, cover the tops of the biscuits with melted butter.

Bake for approximately 15 minutes or until golden brown.

Fried Chicken Nuggets

MAKES 12 PIECES.

2 cups flour
3 teaspoons paprika
1 teaspoon salt
1 teaspoon garlic powder
1 teaspoon ground black pepper
2 eggs
1/2 cup milk
2 pounds boneless chicken
    breasts, washed and dried
4 tablespoons unsalted butter
8 tablespoons vegetable oil

In a small bowl, combine the flour, paprika, salt, garlic powder, and pepper.

In a separate bowl, beat the eggs. Add the milk. Lay the chicken breasts on a cutting board and apart so they lay flat. Cut the breasts into 2-inch-square pieces.

Heat the butter and oil in a skillet until hot. While the skillet is heating, dip the chicken pieces first in the egg mixture and then coat with the flour mixture. Place the nuggets in the hot skillet and cook until golden brown on each side, about 5 minutes. Remove from the skillet and place on paper towel.

To assemble the sandwiches, cut the biscuits in half. Butter each side lightly. Place a Chicken Nugget on each of the biscuit bottoms. Replace the biscuit tops.

NOTE: These can be put together earlier in the day, refrigerated, and reheated in a microwave on high for approximately 30 seconds, or warmed in a 325°F oven, loosely covered with aluminum foil, for approximately 10 minutes.

CAJUN SHRIMP SANDWICHES

MAKES 12 PIECES.

1/8 teaspoon onion powder
1/8 teaspoon garlic powder
1/8 teaspoon cayenne pepper
1/8 teaspoon ground black pepper
1/4 teaspoon paprika
1/4 teaspoon salt
1 tablespoon unsalted butter
1 cup fresh tiny shrimp, peeled,
    cooked, and drained
1 teaspoon grated orange peel
6 thin slices white bread
Unsalted butter

Combine all the seasonings and set aside.

Heat the butter in a skillet until hot and foamy. Pour in the seasonings and cook at medium-high heat for 1 minute. Add the shrimp and orange peel and cook until all the liquid is absorbed, about 2 to 3 minutes. Cool to room temperature.

Spread each slice of bread with a thin coating of butter.

Divide the shrimp mixture between 3 of the bread slices. Top the sandwiches with the remaining bread. Trim the crusts. Cut each sandwich into 4 pieces.

NOTE: If you cannot find fresh tiny shrimp, it is best to buy them frozen rather than canned.

Cajun Shrimp Sandwiches and Sour Cream Sugar Cookies.

POTATO SALAD IN CUCUMBER COMPOTES

MAKES 6 COMPOTES.

1 hard-boiled egg, peeled
2 cups cooked potato
 (approximately 2 large
 potatoes), medium diced
1 cup mashed potato
 (approximately 1 large
 potato)
½ cup finely chopped sweet
 pickles
1 finely chopped scallion
1½ cups mayonnaise
½ teaspoon prepared yellow
 mustard
½ teaspoon celery seed
 Salt (to taste)
1 cucumber, approximately 6
 inches in circumference,
 peeled
 Paprika

Put the egg in a medium-size bowl and finely chop. Add the potatoes, pickles, and scallion to the egg and mix very well.

In a small bowl, mix together the mayonnaise, mustard, celery seed, and salt to taste. Pour this mixture over the potatoes. Using a fork, blend the salad and dressing together. Don't be shy about whipping vigorously with your fork, as this is a creamy potato salad. Chill well before serving (approximately 2 hours).

To assemble, cut 6 1-inch thick slices from the cucumber. With the small end of a melon baller, hollow out the cucumber slices, making sure to leave the walls solid and enough on the bottom to sustain the filling. Fill the hole with 1½ teaspoons of potato salad. The filling will come up over the top, so mound it nicely. Sprinkle each slice with paprika.

NOTE: Because biscuits and muffins are so filling, we make a smaller number of compotes (1 per person). There is enough potato salad to increase this number if you choose, simply by cutting additional cucumber slices.

HAM SALAD IN CORN MUFFIN CUPS

MAKES 6 MUFFIN SANDWICHES.

Corn Muffins

MAKES APPROXIMATELY
1 DOZEN MUFFINS.

1 cup flour
1 cup cornmeal
3 tablespoons sugar
1 tablespoon baking powder
1 teaspoon salt
1 egg
1 cup milk
4 tablespoons melted, unsalted
 butter, cooled to room
 temperature

Preheat oven to 350°F.

Mix the dry ingredients together in a bowl.

In a separate bowl, beat the egg, then beat in the milk. Add the egg mixture to the dry ingredients, mixing until well blended. Pour in the melted butter, beating until it is incorporated into the mixture.

Fill 12 greased muffin cups one half full. Bake in the preheated oven 15 to 20 minutes or until the muffins are golden brown. Cool.

These muffins can be made the day before, and stored in an airtight container, or wrapped in plastic wrap.

Ham Salad

MAKES 1⅓ CUPS.

1 cup cooked ham, medium
 diced
¼ cup red bell pepper, finely
 diced
1 tablespoon scallion, finely
 sliced
4 tablespoons mayonnaise
1 tablespoon honey mustard
2 green olives

Place the ham, bell pepper, and scallion in a bowl and toss to combine. Add the mayonnaise and mustard. Mix well.

This salad lasts well in the refrigerator for 5 days.

To assemble, scoop out the center and sides of each muffin with a melon baller or teaspoon to make a cup. Be careful not to scoop out too much or the muffin will collapse; you want to be able to hold each muffin securely in your hand with no breakage. Fill the muffins with the ham salad. Cut 2 green olives into 3 slices each. Place 1 slice in the center of each muffin.

Potato Salad in Cucumber Compotes, Ham Salad in Corn Muffin Cup, and Fried Chicken 'n' Biscuits.

Luscious Coconut Cake decorated with Strawberries.

COCONUT CAKE

MAKES 1 9-INCH LAYER CAKE.

This is a great example of an "old-time" cake.

Summer Sponge Cake

MAKES 2 9-INCH LAYERS.

1 cup flour
½ teaspoon baking powder
½ teaspoon salt
6 large egg yolks
1 cup sugar
1 tablespoon vanilla
6 large egg whites
⅛ teaspoon cream of tartar
6 tablespoons coconut milk or coconut drink

Preheat oven to 350° F.

In a small bowl, combine the flour, baking powder, and salt. Sift. In a large bowl, beat the egg yolks and ½ cup of the sugar until the mixture is light in color and very thick. (The batter should fall in ribbons when the beater is lifted.) Beat the vanilla into the egg yolks.

In another bowl, beat the egg whites with the cream of tartar until soft peaks start to form. Gradually add the remaining sugar and beat until the egg whites are stiff. Fold the egg whites into the egg yolks, alternating with the dry ingredients.

Divide the batter between 2 greased 9-inch cake pans. Bake for 25 to 30 minutes or until golden brown and a toothpick inserted in the center comes out clean. Remove from the oven and let sit in the pans on cooling racks for 5 minutes.

Remove from pans and let cool completely.

When the cakes are cool, spread 3 tablespoons of coconut milk or drink on each layer and let sit until absorbed.

Boiled Frosting

MAKES 4 CUPS.

1½ cups milk
½ cup butter
1 cup shortening (such as Crisco)
2 cups sugar
1 teaspoon vanilla
1 7-ounce package sweetened coconut
7 large strawberries

In a saucepan, heat the milk to boiling. Cool.

In a large bowl, combine butter, shortening, and sugar, beating for 5 minutes until light and fluffy. Slowly pour the milk into the bowl, beating while you do, and continue beating for an additional 5 minutes. Add the vanilla, beating for 2 additional minutes.

NOTE: This is a wonderful frosting that holds up exceptionally well on hot days.

To assemble the cake, place 1 layer on a plate or serving platter. Frost the top of the layer with 1 cup of Boiled Frosting. Place the second layer on top of the first. Frost the cake with the remaining frosting. Sprinkle the top and sides of the cake with all of the coconut.

Cut 6 strawberries in half and place evenly around the rim of the cake. Holding the seventh strawberry in your hand,

hull side down, cut slices to three-quarters of the way down. Fan out the strawberry in the center of the cake. Serve.

PECAN SCONES

MAKES APPROXIMATELY
10 TO 12 SCONES.

2 cups flour
¼ cup sugar
2 teaspoons baking powder
1 teaspoon salt
3 tablespoons unsalted butter, cold
¾ cup milk
1 egg
½ cup chopped pecans, medium chopped
1 egg yolk
2 tablespoons cold water

Preheat oven to 350° F.

Sift dry ingredients together. Using a pastry blender or 2 knives, cut butter into dry ingredients until mixture is crumbly. Beat milk and egg together. Add pecans. Pour into the dry ingredients and stir.

Prepare a flat surface by flouring it well (the slightly wet dough will absorb the flour quickly). On the flat surface, knead the dough briefly (once or twice) and pat it until it is ¾-inch thick. Cut out the scones with a 2½-inch biscuit cutter and place on a greased baking sheet.

Beat the egg yolk with the cold water. Using a pastry brush, glaze each scone with this mixture. Bake for 25 to 30 minutes or until golden brown. Serve hot or cold with jam and clotted cream, if desired.

SOUR CREAM SUGAR COOKIES

MAKES APPROXIMATELY
3 DOZEN COOKIES.

1 cup shortening (such as Crisco)
2 cups sugar
2 eggs, slightly beaten
½ teaspoon baking soda, dissolved in 1 cup sour cream
6 cups all-purpose flour, approximately
2 teaspoons baking powder
¼ cup golden raisins
Sugar

Preheat oven to 425° F.

Cream shortening. Add the sugar gradually, beating until fluffy. Add eggs and baking soda dissolved in sour cream. Sift together the 5½ cups of flour and the baking powder. Add to the shortening mixture and blend well to make a very wet dough.

Flour a flat surface well and place dough on it. Add enough flour (approximately ½ cup) for the dough to be malleable. Knead quickly. Roll out the dough until it is ¼-inch thick. Cut out circles with a 3-inch round cookie cutter and place them on a greased cookie sheet. Place 3 raisins in the center of each cookie and sprinkle the cookie with a small amount of sugar, approximately ½ teaspoon per cookie. Bake for 10 to 15 minutes or until the cookies are puffed and brown on the bottom and edges. Cool on a rack. Store in an airtight container. These are best if eaten within a week.

CHAPTER SIX

HIGH TEA

Shepherd's Pie

Raisin and Onion Chutney

Strawberry-Raspberry Cobbler

English Breakfast Tea (or your choice)

Serves 6.

H IGH TEA IS A MEAL THAT OCCURS BETWEEN FIVE AND SIX P.M. IN Victorian times it was known as the working man's Tea. It was a convenient time, after work and before an early bedtime, for a hardy meal. Its hardiness distinguishes High Tea from Afternoon Tea. High Tea is the equivalent of supper.

There are no hard and fast rules regarding the bill of fare. In England it can be as simple as a "fry up," but often extends to meat pies, slices of roast, vegetables, and casseroles. There are loaves of fresh bread, wedges of cheese, condiments, and cakes. People have a tendency to empty the larder and the meal often becomes a patchwork quilt of food.

Our High Tea would be best as supper in the fall or winter. It is a warm, cozy meal that provides comfort and nourishment against a cold, rainy, or snowy day.

It can all be done the day before. In fact, the Shepherd's Pie tastes better the next day. Warm it in the oven or heat it in the microwave before serving. Buy the bread and pop it into a hot oven ten minutes before you serve the meal. The green salad we leave to you. A combination of your favorite greens and a simple dressing will do nicely.

While everyone is eating the main course, put the cobbler in a low oven and let it warm. We serve both of the "afters" at the same time, creating a large, informal last course. We suggest pears, apples, and a wedge of sharp cheddar cheese. Place both the fruit and cheese on a cheese board with a small selection of plain crackers. Give everyone a fresh plate and let them serve themselves. One final word about High Tea: Cups of tea are served with and throughout the meal, so get the kettle boiling and keep the brew coming.

SHEPHERD'S PIE

MAKES 1 10-INCH PIE.

Crust and topping
- 5 cups mashed potatoes (approximately 5 potatoes)
- 1 egg yolk
- 1 tablespoon melted unsalted butter

Filling
- 2 tablespoons unsalted butter
- 1 tablespoon vegetable oil
- 1 clove garlic, minced
- 1/2 cup finely diced shallots
- 2 cups clean, dry, sliced mushrooms
- 1 10-ounce package frozen spinach, thawed, and squeezed dry
- 1/2 pound ground beef
- 1/2 pound ground pork
- 1/2 pound ground lamb
- Salt (to taste)
- Pepper (to taste)
- 3 tablespoons flour
- 1 1/4 cups chicken broth
- 1/4 cup white wine or vermouth
- 1/2 teaspoon dry tarragon

Preheat oven to 350°F.

Coat the inside of a 10-inch deep dish pie plate with cooking spray.

Mix together 2 cups of the mashed potatoes with the egg yolk. Spoon this mixture into the pie plate, spreading it evenly over the bottom and sides of the plate. You may find it helpful to wet the spoon with water as you spread the potatoes.

Place the pie plate into the oven and cook for 15 minutes. Remove and let cool as you continue to work on the filling.

Melt butter and the vegetable oil in a skillet over medium-high heat until hot.

Add the garlic and shallots to the pan and cook until translucent. Sprinkle in the mushrooms. Mix well with the garlic and shallots and continue to cook until the mushrooms begin to brown.

While the mushrooms cook, put the squeezed spinach into a medium-size bowl and flake with a fork until it is well separated.

When the mushrooms are browned, remove the vegetables from the pan and add to the spinach. Set aside.

Return the pan to the heat and crumble in the beef, pork, and lamb; cook until brown. Season with salt and pepper.

Remove the meat from the pan and add to the spinach mixture, being careful to leave the drippings in the pan. Keeping the heat medium-high, whisk the flour into the drippings.

Pour the broth and wine into the roux, whisking continuously until you have a thick, smooth gravy. Add the tarragon, and season with salt and pepper. Pour over the meat and spinach mixture, mixing well.

To assemble, spoon the meat mixture into the pie plate, packing it down well. Dot the remaining mashed potatoes over the top of the meat. Use a spoon to smooth it out, making sure the entire top of the dish is covered with the potatoes. Brush on the melted butter. Furrow the top of the pie with a fork.

Place in the preheated oven and bake for 45 minutes until the top is brown. Let sit for 10 minutes before serving.

RAISIN AND ONION CHUTNEY

MAKES 1 CUP.

2	tablespoons unsalted butter
2	cups thinly sliced onion
1½	cups chicken broth
3	teaspoons honey
½	cup golden raisins
	Salt (to taste)

Melt butter in a medium-size skillet. Add the onion and cook over medium-high heat until translucent and beginning to brown, about 5 minutes. Pour in the chicken broth and honey, and cook, covered, until most of the liquid has evaporated and the mixture has thickened, about 10 to 15 minutes.

Add the raisins and continue to cook until they have plumped, about 5 minutes. Season with salt.

Serve warm or at room temperature. The chutney should last in the refrigerator for at least 1 week.

This is a wonderful accompaniment for the Shepherd's Pie as well as other types of poultry and meat.

Raisin and Onion Chutney.

Shepherd's Pie, cheeses, and English Breakfast Tea.

STRAWBERRY-RASPBERRY COBBLER

SERVES 6.

³/₄ cup unsalted butter, at room
temperature
1¹/₂ cups sugar
1¹/₂ cups all-purpose flour
3 cups fresh or frozen
raspberries
2 teaspoons cornstarch
¹/₄ teaspoon salt
4 cups fresh strawberries,
washed and hulled
1 tablespoon fresh lemon juice
¹/₈ cup sugar mixed with
1 teaspoon cinnamon

Cream the butter in a medium-size bowl until light. Gradually add ³/₄ cup of the sugar and beat until light and fluffy. Gently mix in the flour until well blended.

Take a sheet of aluminum foil, and with a knife point, gently mark out an 8-inch square. Lay the dough within this area and pat out evenly with your hand until you have an 8-inch by 8-inch square of dough. Fold the excess foil over the square and place in the refrigerator until cold and firm.

While the dough is chilling, place 1 cup of the raspberries in a small bowl and crush.

Combine the remaining sugar, cornstarch, salt, and the crushed raspberries in a medium-size saucepan.

Heat the mixture over medium heat, stirring constantly, until boiling. Add the strawberries and continue to boil until the mixture has thickened, approximately 5 minutes. Let cool to room temperature.

Preheat oven to 375°F.

Mix the remaining 2 cups of raspberries and lemon juice into the fruit mixture.

Pour the fruit into a greased 9-inch square baking dish.

Remove the crust from the refrigerator, unwrap it, and carefully place on top of the fruit. Sprinkle the sugar and cinnamon mixture evenly over the crust.

Bake for 35 to 45 minutes or until the crust is golden brown and the fruit is bubbling.

Serve warm or at room temperature with heavy cream or ice cream.

Strawberry-Raspberry Cobbler served with whipped cream.

CHAPTER SEVEN

THANKSGIVING TEA

Turkey and Stuffing Sandwiches

Turkey Sandwiches with Basil Mayonnaise

Red Cabbage and Bacon Vinaigrette Tarts

Cranberry Scones

Gingerbread with Fruit Sauce

Assam Tea (or your choice)

Serves 6.

THANKSGIVING IS A SPECIAL HOLIDAY THAT EMPHASIZES FOOD AND THE communion that comes with a shared meal. We love the idea of a day set aside for appreciation and thanks. The traditional Thanksgiving meal is one we look forward to all year. Outside it may be cold and crisp; inside, the warmth and the smell of roasting turkey wafts through the house.

The curious thing about Thanksgiving is, while we look forward to the dinner with all the trimmings, and are always stuffed at the end of it, what we really want is the next meal. The one made with the leftovers. This is the time when we can go into the kitchen and use food that has already been prepared to create another meal. It is a perfect scenario for a Tea.

A Thanksgiving Tea provides a wonderful opportunity to retain our sense of the holiday without having to spend several more hours cooking. Everything in this Tea, except for the clotted cream and the tea, comes from the main holiday meal or can be made a day or two in advance. You might even want to incorporate the cabbage and bacon vinaigrette into your Thanksgiving dinner. Similarly, if you want to delete or change some items (for instance, serving your pies instead of gingerbread), do so. Remember, these are just suggestions.

RED CABBAGE AND BACON VINAIGRETTE TARTS

MAKES 6 TARTS.

Cheese Tart Shells

MAKES APPROXIMATELY 12 SHELLS.

2 cups all-purpose flour
1/4 teaspoon salt
1/2 cup sharp cheddar cheese, firmly packed
2/3 cup shortening, chilled
1/4 cup ice water

Preheat oven to 350°F.

Combine the flour, salt, and cheese in a large bowl. Using a pastry blender or 2 knives, cut in shortening until the mixture resembles a coarse meal. Sprinkle ice water over the meal, a tablespoon at a time, tossing with a fork until a dough is formed.

Place on a floured surface and roll out very thin to 1/8 inch. Cut 4-inch circles out of the dough. Drape the circles over the underside cups of a muffin tin. Leave an empty space between the circles so that the dough has room to bake, and the circles are not crowded.

Press gently with your hand, conforming the dough to the cup shape. Prick with a fork.

Bake for 10 to 15 minutes or until the cup is starting to brown on the outside. To allow for spacing, you will have to do at least 2 batches. Cool on a rack.

The shells can be stored in an airtight container for at least 2 days.

NOTE: The tarts will look prettier if you use a cutter with a crimped edge when cutting out the circles.

Red Cabbage and Bacon Vinaigrette

MAKES 2 1/2 CUPS.

2 cups grated red cabbage
4 strips crispy bacon, crumbled
2 thinly sliced scallions
1/2 cup cider vinegar
1/4 cup vegetable oil
1 tablespoon sugar
2 teaspoons bacon drippings
1 teaspoon celery seed
Salt (to taste)
Freshly ground pepper (to taste)
1 ounce Swiss cheese, cut into 12 thin strips (optional)

Combine the cabbage, bacon, and scallions in a medium-size bowl. Toss well.

In a small microwaveable bowl, combine the rest of the ingredients, except the salt and pepper and cheese. Heat the dressing in a microwave on high for 1 1/2 minutes.

Stir the dressing and pour over the slaw. Season with salt and pepper. Toss to combine.

The slaw can be served at room temperature or chilled.

This will last, well covered, in the refrigerator for 3 days.

To assemble the tarts, fill each shell with 3 tablespoons of the red cabbage and bacon vinaigrette. Place 2 strips of Swiss cheese crisscrossed over the top of each tart. Best served at room temperature.

NOTE: If you don't have a microwave, heat the ingredients in a small saucepan over low heat until warm.

TURKEY AND STUFFING SANDWICHES

MAKES 24 PIECES.

12 thin slices wheat bread
    Unsalted butter
 6 thin slices turkey breast
 6 tablespoons stuffing
 6 teaspoons cranberry sauce

Spread each slice of bread with a thin coating of butter.

Lay a slice of turkey on 6 slices of bread. Spread a tablespoon of stuffing on each slice of turkey, then spoon a teaspoon of cranberry sauce over the stuffing. Top the sandwiches with the remaining bread.

Trim the crusts. Cut each sandwich into 4 pieces.

Red Cabbage and Bacon Vinaigrette Tarts.

TURKEY SANDWICHES WITH BASIL MAYONNAISE

MAKES 12 PIECES.

1 pint (16 fluid ounces)
   mayonnaise
1 cup firmly packed fresh basil
   leaves, washed and dried
2 medium cloves garlic, peeled
Unsalted butter
6 thin slices white bread
3 thin slices leftover turkey

Put mayonnaise, basil, and garlic in a blender or a food processor fitted with the metal blade. Process until pureed, approximately 1 minute. Pour the mixture back into the mayonnaise jar. Refrigerate until chilled, at least 1 hour. This mayonnaise should keep in the refrigerator at least 2 weeks and will surely last as long as your turkey does.

To assemble the sandwiches, spread each slice of bread with a thin coating of butter. Lay a slice of turkey on 3 slices of bread. Spread 1 tablespoon of Basil Mayonnaise on each slice of turkey. Cover the sandwich with the remaining bread. Trim the crusts. Cut each sandwich into 4 pieces.

NOTE: If you cannot find fresh basil, substitute 3 tablespoons of pesto for the basil and garlic. Pesto generally can be found in the refrigerated or freezer section of most grocery stores.

CRANBERRY SCONES

MAKES APPROXIMATELY 10 SCONES.

$3/4$ cup fresh cranberries
  1 cup boiling water
  2 cups flour
$1/2$ cup sugar
  2 teaspoons baking powder
  1 teaspoon salt
  3 tablespoons unsalted butter,
     cold
  1 egg
$3/4$ cup milk
  1 egg yolk
  2 tablespoons cold water

Coarsely chop the cranberries. Cover them with the boiling water and let sit for an hour. Drain off all the liquid.

Sift the dry ingredients together. Using a pastry blender or 2 knives, cut the butter into the dry ingredients until the mixture is crumbly.

Beat the egg and milk together. Pour into the dry ingredients, stirring until a dough is formed. Add the cranberries, mixing well.

Preheat oven to 350°F.

Using an ice cream scoop, form the scones, and place on a greased baking sheet.

Beat the egg yolk with the cold water. Using a pastry brush, glaze each scone with this mixture. Bake for 25 to 30 minutes or until golden brown.

Serve hot or cold with jam and clotted cream, if desired.

GINGERBREAD

MAKES 1 9-INCH LAYER;
6 TO 8 SLICES.

$1/2$ cup butter
$1/2$ cup plus 2 tablespoons sugar
  2 eggs
  1 cup dark molasses
$2^{1}/2$ cups sifted all-purpose flour
  1 teaspoon cinnamon
  1 teaspoon ground cloves
  1 teaspoon ground ginger
  1 teaspoon allspice
  1 teaspoon baking soda
     dissolved in 1 cup boiling
     coffee and cooled to room
     temperature

Preheat oven to 350°F.

Cream the butter. Add $1/2$ cup sugar, eggs, and molasses in that order, beating well after each addition.

Sift together the flour and spices. Add the flour mixture one-third at a time, alternating with the coffee, one-third at a time. Mix until smooth.

Pour into a greased 9-inch cake pan. Sprinkle the top of the batter with the remaining 2 tablespoons sugar.

Bake for 45 minutes to 1 hour. Serve hot or cold.

Cranberry Scones and Gingerbread with Fruit Sauce garnished with fruit and whipped cream.

Fruit Sauce

MAKES APPROXIMATELY 1 CUP.

1 **cup sugar**
1 **cup unsweetened juice
(apple, raspberry-apple, or
cranberry-raspberry)**

Combine the sugar and juice in a medium-size saucepan and heat on high until the sugar has dissolved and the mixture starts to boil.

Turn the heat down to medium and cook, stirring constantly, for 10 minutes until the mixture thickens or until 221°F is reached on a candy thermometer. Pour into a microwave-glass container. Cool, cover, and refrigerate.

The sauce can be served warm or cold.

To warm, heat in a microwave for 15 to 30 seconds. This sauce will last in the refrigerator for at least 2 weeks.

NOTE: This sauce has a tendency to become hard when it is cooled if it has been cooked just a little bit too long. To remedy this, heat in a microwave on high for 1 to 2 minutes.

If you don't have a microwave, place the container in a saucepan that is half full of hot water and heat the container over medium heat until the sauce is warm, about 15 minutes.

To serve, spoon the Fruit Sauce over each slice of Gingerbread, then place a spoonful of whipped cream on the side.

CHAPTER EIGHT

CHRISTMAS TEA

Black Forest Ham Sandwiches

Cucumber Sandwiches

Egg Mayonnaise and Watercress Sandwiches

Stilton, Walnut, and Pear Sandwiches

Jane Mudry's Christmas Cookies

Fruit and Nut Scones

Mary's Almond Mocha Cake

Darjeeling Tea (or your choice)

Serves 6.

THE HALLS ARE DECKED, THE TREE IS TRIMMED, AND CAROLERS ARE singing; holiday spirit abounds. Christmas day is a wonderful occasion for a Tea. The decor is already in place, the ambience established; breakfast and Christmas dinner were consumed hours ago. A Tea is the perfect answer for those who grow peckish as evening draws nigh.

A Christmas Day Tea is very easy to put together. The baking can be done in advance with the rest of your holiday baking. The sandwiches can be prepared in the morning, wrapped well, and placed in the refrigerator until needed. One hour before the Tea, prepare the clotted cream (this gives it time to set and chill). When you are ready to serve, place the sandwiches and desserts on platters, set out the tea things, warm the scones, and brew the tea.

You may find, as we have, that your guests are so delighted by Christmas Tea, that it will become a tradition in your home.

We suggest the following menu for your Tea. Use it, make substitutes, or design your own.

BLACK FOREST HAM SANDWICHES

MAKES 12 PIECES.

8 thin slices dark bread
Unsalted butter
4 slices Black Forest ham
Honey mustard

Spread the top and bottom of each slice of bread with a thin coating of butter.

On 4 slices of the bread, place a ham slice, folding the ham to conform to the bread size and keeping in mind that the crusts will be trimmed off. Spread a thin coating of honey mustard on each slice of ham. Top each sandwich with the remaining bread. Trim the crusts. Cut each sandwich into 3 parallel pieces.

CUCUMBER SANDWICHES

MAKES 12 PIECES.

6 thin slices white bread
Unsalted butter
1/2 medium cucumber, peeled and thinly sliced
Salt (to taste)
Pepper (to taste)

Spread each slice of bread with a thin coating of butter. Place the cucumber slices on 3 slices of bread, making sure the bread is well covered (approximately 6 to 8 slices of cucumber per piece of bread). Season each sandwich with salt and pepper. Cover with the remaining slices of buttered bread. Trim the crusts. Cut each sandwich into 4 pieces.

EGG MAYONNAISE AND WATERCRESS SANDWICHES

MAKES 12 PIECES.

2 hard-boiled eggs
1 1/2 tablespoons mayonnaise
1/8 cup watercress, washed and picked from stems
Salt (to taste)
Pepper (to taste)
4 thin slices white bread
Unsalted butter
4 thin slices wheat bread

Finely chop the hard-boiled eggs. Whisk the mayonnaise and cream cheese together until smooth. Add this mixture to the eggs and mix until well blended. Fold in the watercress. Season with salt and pepper.

Spread each slice of the white bread with a thin coating of butter. Spread the egg salad evenly on the bread. Butter the wheat bread and place a slice on top of each sandwich. Trim the crusts. Cut each sandwich into 3 parallel pieces.

STILTON, WALNUT, AND PEAR SANDWICHES

MAKES 12 PIECES.

1/4   **pound English Stilton cheese**
1/2   **cup walnuts**
1/2   **ripe pear, cored**
6   **thin slices wheat bread**
Unsalted butter

Crumble the cheese and let it soften. While the cheese is softening, toast the walnuts under the broiler for approximately 8 to 10 minutes or until golden brown. Cool and chop very fine.

Slice the pear into 12 thin slices.

Spread each slice of bread with a thin coating of butter.

Divide the cheese equally among 3 slices of the bread and spread it gently. Sprinkle a heaping tablespoon of walnuts over the cheese. Place 4 slices of the pear on each sandwich. Top each sandwich with the remaining bread slices, pressing down firmly.

Trim the crusts. Cut each sandwich into 4 pieces.

Decorated Christmas Cookies (see recipe on page 66).

Jane Mudry's Christmas Cookies

MAKES 1 TO 1½ DOZEN COOKIES.

Cookie Dough
- 1 cup unsalted butter
- ½ cup sugar
- 1 egg
- 2 teaspoons vanilla
- 2½ cups sifted all-purpose flour
- ½ teaspoon baking powder
- ⅛ teaspoon salt

Frosting
- 1 tablespoon unsalted butter
- 1½ cups confectioner's sugar
- ½ teaspoon vanilla
- Milk

Preheat oven to 350°F.

To make the cookies, cream the butter and sugar together. Add the egg and vanilla and mix well. Sift together the dry ingredients and slowly add to the butter mixture. Combine until a dough is formed. If the dough is too wet, add up to an additional ½ cup of flour. Put one-quarter of the dough onto a floured surface. Sprinkle the top of the dough with flour. Using a rolling pin, roll out the dough until it is ⅛-inch thick. Cut out desired shapes with cookie cutters. Repeat this procedure until all the dough has been used.

Bake on ungreased cookie sheets for 8 to 10 minutes or until lightly browned on the edges. Cool and frost.

To prepare the frosting, cream together the butter and sugar. Add the vanilla and mix well. Pour in milk, a teaspoon at a time,

until you have a spreadable consistency. Frost the cooled cookies and decorate.

This recipe can be made several hours before the cookies, but should be kept in the refrigerator. You will have to allow time for the frosting to soften for use.

Fruit and Nut Scones

MAKES APPROXIMATELY 12 SCONES.

- 3 cups flour
- ¼ cup sugar
- ½ teaspoon salt
- 1 tablespoon baking powder
- 5 tablespoons unsalted butter
- 2 eggs
- 1¼ cups milk
- ½ cup walnuts, chopped medium-fine
- ¼ cup currants
- 1 egg yolk
- 2 tablespoons cold water

Preheat oven to 350°F.

Sift the dry ingredients together. Using a pastry blender or 2 knives, cut the butter into the dry ingredients until crumbly. Beat the eggs and milk together. Combine the walnuts with the currants. Pour the egg mixture into the dry ingredients, stirring until a dough is formed. Fold in the walnuts and currants.

Using an ice cream scoop, form the scones and place on a greased baking sheet. Beat the egg yolk with the cold water. Using a pastry brush, glaze each scone with this mixture. Bake for 20 minutes, or until golden brown. Serve hot or cold with jam and clotted cream.

Mary's Almond Mocha Cake

SERVES 12.

Cake
- 2 teaspoons vanilla
- 2 teaspoons water
- 4 large eggs
- ½ cup sugar
- 1 teaspoon salt
- 1 cup sifted all-purpose flour
- 6 tablespoons melted unsalted butter, cooled to room temperature

Frosting
- 4 teaspoons instant coffee granules
- 6 tablespoons hot milk
- 2½ sticks unsalted butter
- 2 teaspoons vanilla

Decorations
- 2½ cups sliced, blanched almonds
- Confectioner's sugar

To make the cake, preheat oven to 325°F.

Butter and flour a 9-inch cake pan.

Mix the vanilla and water together. Combine the eggs, sugar, salt, and vanilla mixture in a bowl and beat on high in a mixer until the batter is white and very thick. (When you lift your beaters from the bowl, the batter should fall in thick folds.)

Gently fold in the flour, then the butter, making sure both are totally incorporated. Do not stir.

Pour into the prepared cake pan and bake for 35 to 40 minutes. The cake is done when it is golden brown and springs to the touch.

Invert the cake onto a rack. When the cake has cooled completely, split it into 2 equal layers.

To make the frosting, dissolve the granules in the hot milk. Cream the butter and sugar until smooth. Mix in the vanilla. Beat in the hot milk and coffee until the frosting is creamy. If necessary, use more milk. Refrigerate the frosting until it becomes firm and spreadable. Frost.

To frost and decorate the cake, first toast the almonds in a hot oven until they are a light golden brown. Cool.

Place 1 layer of the cake on a serving dish. Cover the top of this layer with 1 to 1½ cups of the frosting, spreading evenly. Top this with the second layer and press gently.

Frost the top and sides of the cake with the remaining frosting. Starting at the bottom, press the almond slices into the cake, overlapping the almonds on top of each other, until you reach the top. Continue the same procedure with the top of the cake until all but a 3-inch circle in the center is covered.

Roughly crush the remaining almonds and sprinkle this on the uncovered section. You may find it necessary to place the cake in the refrigerator from time to time while you are decorating with the almonds, because the butter frosting may become too soft and difficult to work with.

Once the cake is completely covered with almonds, dust the top lightly with confectioner's sugar.

Almond Mocha Cake.

CHAPTER NINE

EASTER TEA

Clove Chicken Puffs

Deviled Eggs

Timothy's Chicken Liver Pâté on Toast Rounds

Watercress Sandwiches

Lemon Crisps

Chocolate-Dipped Strawberries

Date-Nut Scones

Fabergé Carrot Cake

Lady Londonderry Tea (or your choice)

Serves 6.

EASTER CELEBRATES NEW LIFE. IT IS A RECOGNITION OF REBIRTH AND flowering and it symbolizes that life comes from life. There can be no more perfect symbol of this regeneration than that of the egg. The egg is the primary Easter symbol in many cultures and is expressed in accordance with their traditions. Some make braided egg breads, some prefer to express themselves in chocolate; the Ukrainians create beautiful eggs using wax dyes and allegorical motifs; and Fabergé raised the egg to its ultimate expression with jewels and precious metals.

Keeping the egg in mind, we created our Easter Tea with deviled eggs as the starting point and extended it to the chicken, keeping the first course and dessert "all in the family." Beyond the Easter symbolism, we included foods that make us think of the freshness of spring. There is a lightness to this Tea that won't interfere with a lamb or ham dinner that may be the traditional main meal in your home on Easter day.

As with many of our other Teas, most of the preparatory work can be done in advance. So don your bonnet and then, in the late afternoon or early evening, make this Easter different by having a Tea.

CLOVE CHICKEN PUFFS

MAKES 12 PUFFS.

Miniature Cream Puff Shells (Pâté à Choux)

MAKES APPROXIMATELY 12 SHELLS.

- ½ **cup water**
- 4 **tablespoons salted butter**
- ½ **cup all-purpose flour**
- 2 **eggs**

Preheat oven to 350°F.

Combine the water and butter in a medium-size saucepan. Bring to a boil. When the butter has melted, turn heat down to low and pour the flour into the pan all at once. Beat the mixture until well combined and the batter comes away from the sides of the pan. Remove from heat.

Break 1 egg into the batter and beat until smooth and glossy. Repeat with the second egg. Drop the batter, by rounded teaspoons, onto a greased baking sheet. Bake for 45 minutes or until puffed and golden. Cool.

These are best if made the day you plan to use them, but they can be stored in a dry, airtight container overnight.

Clove Chicken Salad

MAKES 6 CUPS.

Salad
- 1 **cup walnuts**
- 4 **cups cooked chicken, medium diced**
- 4 **thinly sliced scallions**
- 1 **medium green bell pepper, medium diced**
- 1 **cup golden or brown raisins**
- 1 **teaspoon ground cloves**
- ½ **teaspoon salt**
- ¼ **teaspoon minced fresh ginger**

Dressing
- 1½ **cups mayonnaise**
- 2 **teaspoons ground cloves**
- 2 **tablespoons honey**
- 2 **tablespoons apple cider vinegar**
- ½ **cup milk**

To make the salad, coarsely chop the walnuts. Combine the rest of the ingredients in a large bowl.

In another bowl, whisk together the dressing ingredients. Pour the dressing over the salad and toss to combine, making sure the salad is well mixed. Place in the refrigerator until well chilled, approximately 2 to 3 hours.

To assemble the puffs, cut the top off each shell two-thirds of the way up from the bottom. If necessary, remove the excess dough from the center. Fill the bottom of the shell with 3 tablespoons of Clove Chicken Salad. Replace the tops of each puff. Refrigerate until serving.

Deviled Eggs decorated and garnished with vegetables.

DEVILED EGGS

MAKES 12 HALVES.

❖

6 large eggs, hard-boiled and
  peeled
6 teaspoons minced sweet
  pickles
2¹/₂ teaspoons minced scallions
¹/₂ cup mayonnaise
Salt (to taste)
Pepper (to taste)
Paprika

Cut the eggs in half lengthwise; reserve the halved egg whites.

Place the yolks in a small bowl and mash. Add the pickles and scallions to the mashed yolk, blending with a fork.

Using a fork, whip in the mayonnaise. Season with salt and pepper.

Using either a spoon or a pastry tube, refill the egg whites with the mixture, dividing equally between the 12 halves.

Sprinkle paprika over the top of each egg. Chill and serve. The eggs will not last for more than 24 hours.

VARIATION: Add ¹/₂ teaspoon curry powder (or to taste) to the egg mixture. Fill and chill as directed.

Timothy's Chicken Liver Pâté on Toast Rounds

MAKES 6 ROUNDS.

❋

This pâté recipe has evolved over several years and is the best we have ever tasted.

> 2 medium onions, coarsely chopped
> 4 cloves garlic, coarsely chopped
> 3 tablespoons olive oil
> 8 tablespoons lightly salted butter
> 1 pound chicken livers, rinsed in cold water and drained
> 1 teaspoon dried rosemary
> 2 tablespoons sherry
> 1 hard-boiled egg, finely chopped
> 1/2 cup walnuts, finely chopped
> Salt (to taste)
> Pepper (to taste)
> 3 thin slices white bread
> Butter
> 2 pitted black olives

Sauté the onions and garlic in the olive oil and 2 tablespoons of the butter until translucent. Add the chicken livers and rosemary, cooking on high heat until the livers are lightly browned and most of the liquid has evaporated. Cool to room temperature.

When the liver mixture has cooled, put it into a blender or food processor fitted with the metal blade and purée. Add the sherry and remaining butter to the pureed mixture. Purée again.

Place the pureed mixture in a bowl and fold in the egg and walnuts. The mixture should be the consistency of a thin paste. If it is too thick, add more sherry, 1 tablespoon at a time, to thin. Season with salt and pepper. At this point the pâté can be placed in a mold if you choose to do so. Whether you use a mold or not, put the mixture in the refrigerator until thoroughly chilled. This pâté freezes beautifully, so it can be made well in advance of any party.

To assemble, cut 2 2½-inch rounds from each slice of bread with a cookie cutter. Toast the rounds. Lightly butter each round. Spread 1 generous tablespoon of the Pâté on each round, swirling the spoon as you do so. Cut each olive into three equal pieces. Top each round with an olive piece.

VARIATION:
Put the pâté in a pastry bag and pipe it onto the rounds. You may need to use more pâté depending on the size of the nozzle you choose.

Watercress Sandwiches

MAKES 12 PIECES.

❋

> 6 thin slices white bread
> Unsalted butter
> 1/2 bunch watercress, approximately 20 stems, washed, dried, and leaves picked from stem
> Salt (to taste)
> Pepper (to taste)

Spread each slice of bread with a thin coating of butter.

Divide the watercress between three slices of bread. Season with salt and pepper. Cover the sandwiches with the remaining bread slices, pressing down firmly.

Trim the crusts. Cut each sandwich into 4 pieces.

NOTE: Some people prefer to chop the watercress leaves and spread them on the sandwiches; the option is yours.

Chocolate-Dipped Strawberries

MAKES 12 PIECES.

❋

> 6 to 8 ounces semisweet chocolate
> 12 large strawberries, washed and dried

Melt the chocolate in the top half of a double boiler. Gently holding the hull, dip the strawberries into the chocolate until two-thirds of the strawberry is covered. Place the strawberries on a wax paper–covered plate and refrigerate until set, about 1/2 to 1 hour.

These can be made 24 hours in advance and covered with plastic wrap once the chocolate has set. Leftovers will last for at least 2 days, covered and refrigerated.

LEMON CRISPS

MAKES APPROXIMATELY
3 DOZEN CRISPS.

$3/4$ **cup confectioner's sugar**
$2/3$ **cup unsalted butter, at room temperature**
$1/4$ **cup fresh lemon juice**
  2 **tablespoons grated lemon zest**
$13/4$ **cups all-purpose flour**

In a medium-size bowl, beat the sugar and butter until light and fluffy. Add the lemon juice and zest, beating until blended.

Gradually add the flour, beating until smooth. Cover with plastic wrap and refrigerate until chilled, approximately 1 hour.

Preheat oven to 325°F.

Lay the dough on a lightly floured surface. Roll it out until it is about $1/8$-inch thick. Cut out with a 2-inch heart or circle cutter and place on an ungreased cookie sheet 1 inch apart. Bake for 20 to 25 minutes or until slightly golden brown around the edges. Cool. Store in an airtight container. These crisps will stay fresh for a week and freeze wonderfully for up to 2 months.

Plate of Lemon Crisps and Chocolate Dipped Strawberries with fruit and mint candy.

DATE-NUT SCONES

MAKES APPROXIMATELY 10 SCONES.

  2 **cups flour**
$1/4$ **cup sugar**
  2 **teaspoons baking powder**
  1 **teaspoon salt**
  3 **tablespoons unsalted butter, cold**
$3/4$ **cup milk**
  1 **egg**
$1/2$ **cup minced dates**
$1/2$ **cup chopped walnuts**
  1 **egg yolk**
  2 **tablespoons cold water**

Preheat oven to 350°F.

Sift the dry ingredients together. Using a pastry blender or 2 knives, cut the butter into the dry ingredients until the mixture is crumbly. Beat the milk and egg together. Pour into the dry ingredients and stir until well blended. Add the dates and nuts, stirring until they are incorporated into the mixture.

Prepare a flat surface by flouring it well (the dough will be slightly wet and will absorb the flour quickly). Place the dough on the flat surface. Knead briefly (once or twice) and pat the dough until it is $3/4$-inch thick. Cut out the scones with a $21/2$-inch biscuit center and place on a greased baking sheet.

Beat the egg yolk with the cold water. Using a pastry brush, glaze each scone with this mixture. Bake for 25 to 30 minutes or until golden brown.

Serve hot or cold, with jam and clotted cream, if desired.

FABERGÉ CARROT CAKE

MAKES 1 EGG CAKE

Cream Cheese Frosting

MAKES APPROXIMATELY 4 TO 4¹/₂ CUPS.

1 **pound cream cheese, at room temperature**
¹/₂ **cup unsalted butter, at room temperature**
1 **tablespoon vanilla**
1 **1-pound box confectioner's sugar**

In a large bowl, cream the cream cheese and butter until light and fluffy. Beat in the vanilla until well blended. Add the sugar, beating until frosting is formed. Refrigerate the frosting until chilled and firm.

Carrot Egg Cake

MAKES 1 CAKE

2 **cups all-purpose flour**
1 **teaspoon baking powder**
1 **teaspoon baking soda**
1 **teaspoon salt**
1 **teaspoon cinnamon**
1 **teaspoon nutmeg**
1¹/₂ **cups vegetable oil**
1³/₄ **cups sugar**
4 **eggs, at room temperature**
3¹/₂ **cups grated carrot, approximately 1¹/₂ to 2 pounds**
1 **cup finely chopped walnuts**

Preheat oven to 325°F.

In a medium-size bowl, combine the dry ingredients and spices. Sift the mixture once.

In a larger bowl, beat the oil and sugar until blended.

Add the eggs, one at a time, beating well.

Add the dry ingredients and beat until well incorporated. Blend in the carrots and nuts.

Prepare 1 set of egg cake pans by coating well with cooking spray. Set the egg halves on their stands and place on a baking sheet. Pour the batter into the egg pans, dividing evenly between the 2 pans. Gently put the baking sheet into the oven.

Bake the cakes for approximately 45 minutes to 1 hour or until a toothpick inserted in the center comes out clean. Cool in the pans.

To assemble the cakes, slice a thin layer off the bottom of 1 Carrot Cake egg half. (This will create balance and allow the cake to stand.) Place the one-half egg cake layer on a large plate or platter. Spread ³/₄ cup of Cream Cheese Frosting on the top of the half. Now place the other half of the cake on top, creating a whole egg.

To frost and decorate, decide what color you want the egg to be. Create the color using approximately 1¹/₂ cups of Cream Cheese Frosting and food coloring. Frost the entire egg with this color, smoothing it as you frost.

Put ³/₄ cup Cream Cheese Frosting in a small bowl. Drop green and yellow food coloring into the frosting at a ratio of 3 green drops to 1 yellow drop to create a pistachio green color.

Put this mixture in a pastry tube, fitted with a tip appropriate to your design. Pipe a latticework or basket-weave pattern over the entire egg.

Put ¹/₂ cup Cream Cheese Frosting in a bowl. Add yellow and red drops of food coloring to the frosting at a ratio of 3 red drops to 1 yellow drop to create a salmon color.

Pipe small flower designs at the point where the basket-weave lines intersect.

Chill the cake until the designs have set, approximately 2 to 3 hours.

NOTE: This frosting must be very cold to work well. Return both pastry bag and cake to the refrigerator as necessary.

Decorate the cake any way you want. Another example is to frost the cake in white. Do the basket-weave or latticework pattern in green. Put candied violets in the spaces between the lines and candy silver balls where the lines intersect.

For a nice finishing touch, surround the finished egg with fake grass. Sprinkle jelly beans on the grass for added color, or, for an elegant touch, lay small spring flowers on the grass.

Decorated Fabergé Carrot Cake.

CHAPTER TEN

RUSSIAN TEA

Blinis with Caviar and Sour Cream

Cucumbers and Sour Cream

Smoked Salmon Sandwiches on Dark Bread

Cinnamon Rolls

Russian Tea with Sour Cherry Preserves

Tea Cakes

Russian Spice Cake

Serves 6.

THERE IS A MYSTERY AND FRAGRANCE ABOUT RUSSIA THAT ALWAYS captures our imaginations. It is a land of great palaces, balalaikas being strummed, Fabergé eggs, and caviar; a culture where the exoticism of the East blends with the strength and practicality of the West. This is most apparent in their food. The Russian bill of fare is a hardy one, where breads, soups, and fish provide the sustenance needed to survive the fierce climate.

There are some foods that always make us think of Russia. Blinis with caviar, smoked salmon on dark bread, and richly flavored cakes, all of which are in our Russian Tea menu. The rest of the menu was designed to complement these foods and to help complete a sense of the spicy elegance that is so Russian to us.

While we do suggest that you plan on serving at least two blinis to each guest, we don't tell you how much caviar to use or what kind to buy. In a perfect world, large spoonfuls of Beluga would be ideal, but you may have to temper what is ideal with what is financially practical. And, while we do tell you how to serve tea with preserves, if you think your guests would prefer the more conventional tea with milk, the substitution will work fine. Finally, should you wish to have scones, use the Walnut Scones (recipe on page 40) in place of the Cinnamon Rolls.

This is not a Tea for the middle of summer; late fall or winter is best. If you can, arrange to time the baking of the Cinnamon Rolls with the arrival of your guests. A warm house filled with this aroma will tempt their appetites and establish a mood that will put your Tea on the road to success.

BLINIS WITH CAVIAR AND SOUR CREAM

MAKES APPROXIMATELY 30 BLINIS.

- 1 cup milk
- 1/2 package active dry yeast, approximately 1/2 tablespoon
- 4 large eggs, separated
- 1 cup sifted buckwheat flour
- 1/2 cup white flour
- 1 tablespoon sugar
- 1/2 teaspoon salt
- 3 tablespoons unsalted butter, melted and cooled to room temperature
- 3 tablespoons clarified butter (see NOTE)
- Caviar
- Sour cream
- Chopped fresh dill

Pour the milk into a small saucepan. Scald, then cool to lukewarm. Add the yeast to the milk, stirring until dissolved. Let sit for 10 minutes.

Meanwhile, in a large bowl, beat the egg yolks until thick, approximately 3 to 5 minutes.

Combine the flours, sugar, and salt. Beat into the egg yolks. Add the melted butter, stirring to incorporate. Pour in the yeast mixture, stirring until blended.

Cover the bowl with a clean towel or plastic wrap. Set in a warm place to rise until doubled in size, approximately 1 1/2 hours.

When the batter has doubled in size, beat the egg whites in a separate bowl until stiff. Fold the egg whites into the batter.

Heat a griddle or skillet over medium-high heat until hot. Brush lightly with clarified butter.

Make small pancakes by pouring 1 tablespoon of batter onto the griddle, and spreading slightly with a spoon. Cook for approximately 1 minute or until top is bubbly. Turn the blini over with a spatula and cook for about an additional 30 seconds. Keep in a warm oven while you make the remaining blinis. Brush the griddle with clarified butter as needed.

Blinis are always best if made fresh. If necessary, you can refrigerate them, well wrapped, for up to 3 days. Reheat in a microwave oven on high for 15 seconds or in a warm 325°F oven, covered, for approximately 10 minutes.

To assemble the blinis, place them on a serving tray or arrange them on individual plates.

Using a wooden or bone spoon (metal will react against the caviar) place the caviar in the center of each warm blini. Place a slightly smaller amount of sour cream to the side of the caviar. Lightly sprinkle the sour cream with fresh dill.

We suggest at least 2 blinis per guest. Arrange them so they slightly overlap.

NOTE: When clarifying butter what you are doing is separating the fat from the milk product. To do this, heat the butter in a small saucepan until melted. Skim the foam off the top. Pour out the clear yellow liquid, being careful to leave behind the white sediment on the bottom. The yellow liquid is the clarified butter.

CUCUMBERS AND SOUR CREAM

MAKES 12 PIECES.

4 finely sliced scallions
8 tablespoons sour cream
Salt (to taste)
2 large cucumbers, approximately 7 inches in circumference, peeled
Freshly ground pepper

Mix the scallions and sour cream together. Season with salt.

From the widest parts of the cucumber, cut 6 1-inch thick slices. Using a melon baller, scoop a small amount from the center of each slice.

Fill the scooped-out cucumber slices with the sour cream mix, using approximately 2 teaspoons per slice. Grind the pepper over the slices.

Refrigerate until serving.

SMOKED SALMON SANDWICHES ON DARK BREAD

MAKES 12 PIECES.

2 tablespoons unsalted butter
1/2 teaspoon capers
3 thick slices pumpernickel bread
6 ounces thinly sliced smoked salmon
Chopped fresh dill

Using a fork, mash together the butter and the capers until they are blended and the butter is soft.

Divide this mixture between the 3 slices of bread and spread evenly. Lay 2 ounces of smoked salmon on each slice of bread.

Sprinkle fresh dill over the top of each sandwich.

Cut each sandwich into 4 pieces.

Cinnamon Rolls served with tea.

CINNAMON ROLLS

MAKES APPROXIMATELY 15 ROLLS.

1	1-pound loaf frozen bread dough
10	tablespoons unsalted butter
$^1/_2$	cup light brown sugar
$^1/_2$	cup sugar
$1^1/_2$	teaspoons cinnamon
$^1/_4$	teaspoon ground cloves
$^3/_4$	cup walnut pieces
2	tablespoons honey

Prepare a 12-by-8-by-2-inch baking pan by coating it with cooking spray.

Thaw the dough according to the package instructions. While the bread is thawing, make a paste of 6 tablespoons of the butter, the sugars, and the spices. Melt the remaining butter.

Lay the thawed bread on a lightly floured surface and roll out to a rectangle measuring approximately 15 by 18 inches. Spread the sugar paste evenly on the dough, making sure the entire rectangle is covered. Sprinkle the walnut pieces over the dough.

Starting at one of the 15-inch sides, roll the dough up tightly to form a round tube. Seal the seam along the length of the tube by pinching the dough. Drizzle half the melted butter into the prepared pan. Cut 1-inch slices from the dough tube. Lay slices in the pan, being careful not to crowd them. Cover the baking dish with a cloth and let rise in a warm place until doubled in size, approximately 1 hour.

Preheat oven to 375°F.

Drizzle the remaining melted butter over the uncooked rolls. Do the same with the honey. Bake in the preheated oven for 30 to 45 minutes, or until golden brown and the filling is bubbly. Let sit for 10 minutes. Invert the pan onto a serving platter or plate. The sugary bottom will now be on top.

Serve warm or at room temperature. These rolls reheat beautifully in a microwave on high for 30 seconds or in a 325°F oven, covered with foil, for 10 to 15 minutes.

RUSSIAN TEA WITH SOUR CHERRY PRESERVES

**Sour cherry preserves
1 pot freshly brewed
      Russian Tea
Sugar cubes
Thin lemon slices, cut in half
(optional)**

Place 1 teaspoon of sour cherry preserves in the bottom of each teacup, making sure each cup gets at least 1 whole cherry. Pour the tea over the preserves. Serve.

If you want to be truly authentic, use tea glasses that sit in metal stands.

The Russian tradition is to hold a sugar cube between the teeth as you drink the tea. This is not an absolute rule, but we would advise against putting sugar in the cup and stirring. The preserves sweeten the tea and the idea is to drink it with the cherry surprising the palate at the end. Stirring would disturb this. If you'd like a little extra flavor, add a thin slice of lemon to the drink.

Russian Tea with Sour Cherry Preserves.

81

TEA CAKES

MAKES APPROXIMATELY
3 TO 4 DOZEN CAKES.

1 cup unsalted butter, at room
    temperature
4$^{1}/_{2}$ cups confectioner's sugar
1$^{1}/_{2}$ teaspoons vanilla
2 cups all-purpose flour
$^{1}/_{2}$ teaspoon salt
$^{3}/_{4}$ cup finely chopped walnuts

Preheat oven to 350°F.

Cream butter in a food processor fitted with the metal blade.

Add $^{3}/_{4}$ cup of the sugar and vanilla and process until mixed.

Add flour and salt. Process until blended, but do not overwork. Pour in the nuts and pulse just until they are evenly distributed.

Remove dough from food processor and roll into 1-inch balls. Place the balls on an ungreased cookie sheet and bake until firm and starting to brown on the bottom. Remove from oven.

Carefully roll the hot cookies in confectioner's sugar. Let cool, then roll again.

Stored in an airtight container, these should last 2 weeks.

RUSSIAN SPICE CAKE

MAKES 1 9-INCH LAYER CAKE.

Spice Cake

MAKES 2 9-INCH LAYERS.

2$^{1}/_{2}$ cups self-rising cake flour
2 teaspoons cinnamon
$^{1}/_{2}$ teaspoon nutmeg
$^{1}/_{2}$ teaspoon ground ginger
$^{1}/_{2}$ teaspoon ground cloves
1 teaspoon baking soda
$^{1}/_{2}$ cup shortening (such as
    Crisco)
4 tablespoons butter
$^{3}/_{4}$ cup firmly packed light brown
    sugar
$^{1}/_{2}$ cup sugar
2 eggs
1 cup sour cream
$^{1}/_{2}$ cup milk
$^{3}/_{4}$ cup chopped walnuts, medium
    chopped
$^{3}/_{4}$ cup currants

Preheat oven to 350°F. Grease 2 9-inch cake pans.

Sift the flour with the rest of the dry ingredients and set aside.

In a large bowl, cream the shortening and butter. Add the sugars, beating until light and fluffy. Add the eggs 1 at a time, beating for 1 minute after each egg. Add the flour mixture, one-half at a time, alternating with half of the sour cream until all has been beaten and blended. Pour in the milk and beat until well combined. Add the nuts and currants, beating only to blend thoroughly.

Pour the batter into the prepared cake pans, dividing evenly. Bake for 25 to 35 minutes or until cakes are golden brown and a toothpick inserted in the center comes out clean. Remove to cake racks and cool.

Two-Cream Frosting

MAKES APPROXIMATELY
3$^{1}/_{2}$ TO 4 CUPS.

$^{1}/_{2}$ pound cream cheese, at room
    temperature
6 tablespoons butter, at room
    temperature
$^{1}/_{3}$ cup sour cream
1 teaspoon vanilla
1 1-pound box confectioner's
    sugar
1 cup walnut pieces

In a medium-size mixing bowl, blend the cream cheese and butter until light and fluffy. Add the sour cream and vanilla. Pour in the sugar and beat until frosting is formed. This frosting can be made a day or two in advance, but should be brought to room temperature for easier frosting.

To assemble the cake, place 1 layer on a plate or serving platter. Spread 1 cup of Two-Cream Frosting on the top. Place the second layer over the first. Frost the top and sides of the cake. Sprinkle the walnut pieces over the top. Chill until the frosting sets, approximately 2 hours. Set out $^{1}/_{2}$ hour before serving. Protected with plastic wrap, this cake will stay fresh 3 to 5 days.

Russian Spice Cake decorated with cherries.

CHAPTER ELEVEN

CHINESE TEA

Chinese Pancakes filled with Shredded Chicken in Peanut Sauce

Crescent Moon Melon Slices

Almond Cakes

Sweet and Crunchy Walnuts

Baby Shrimp with Cashews

Sautéed Chinese Vegetables

Oolong Tea (or your choice)

Serves 6.

OVER THE CENTURIES, CHINA HAS GENEROUSLY SHARED THE GIFTS AND benefits of its culture with the rest of the world. The Chinese have given us silk, porcelain, paper, gunpowder, firecrackers, and pasta. China has given us philosophy and blessed us with tea.

Legend has it that the Chinese emperor Shen Nung (28th century B.C.) discovered tea by accident. He always drank boiled water as a way of protecting himself from the prevalent illnesses of the time. One day his servants built the fire for his water using the branches of a nearby tree. Some of the leaves from the branches floated into the boiling water, and the fragrance released caught the emperor's attention. He sipped the hot liquid and was delighted by the flavor. That first sip flowered into tea-drinking ceremonies and traditions that steadily increased in popularity.

We wanted to do a Tea with an Asian flavor. We chose China because their foods are easily adaptable to the Western tea ceremony and it is appropriate to reflect the taste of tea's parent culture.

The pancakes are a wonderful alternative to sandwiches. We suggest you place the fillings on three separate platters surrounded by the pancakes. Be sure to have plenty of pancakes as the fillings go a long way and this combination is very popular. Let the guests fill and make their own pancakes.

The almond cakes are a combination of East and West. They are lighter than most Chinese desserts, many of which are boiled, but forgo the frosted cakiness of the West.

This Tea is simpler and lighter in style than the other Teas in this book, but equally as elegant. Keep this in mind as you arrange your table. One suggestion is to place the pancakes on one side of the tea table and the sweets on the other, with flowers and your teapot occupying the middle. Drinking the delicate oolong tea out of thin China cups is a lovely addition. Play some quiet music in the background. All of this will create an atmosphere of peace and serenity that the Chinese love and your guests will appreciate as an escape from our often hectic world.

FILLED CHINESE PANCAKES

MAKES 18 PANCAKES.

1¼ cups flour
1 teaspoon salt
½ cup boiling water
Sesame oil

In a medium-size bowl, combine flour and salt. Pour the boiling water into the bowl and stir until a dough is formed. Knead the dough for 10 minutes. Place in a bowl, cover with a cloth, and set in a warm place for 45 minutes.

Shape the dough into a tube approximately 9 inches long. Cut into 18 equal ½-inch thick pieces. Roll the pieces into balls. Keep the balls you are not using immediately covered with a damp paper towel. Flatten 2 of the balls at a time into small "pancakes." Place a drop of sesame oil on each pancake and spread evenly over the top. Press the 2 pancakes together, oiled sides touching, to create 1. Roll out the dough until it is very thin and approximately 7 inches in diameter.

Heat a heavy skillet until hot. Rub a small drop of sesame oil onto the bottom of the skillet. Place a pancake in the hot skillet and cook for 30 seconds. Turn the pancake over. When it has puffed, separate the 2 pancakes using your fingers. This is hot work, so be careful.

Place the pancakes on a plate and cover with a damp cloth while you cook the others. If you are eating immediately, spoon filling into the center of the pancake. Fold the bottom flap over the filling. Fold over the sides. If you plan on having the meal later, keep them covered, unfilled, in plastic wrap and reheat in a microwave, 6 at a time (covered loosely with plastic wrap), for 30 seconds on high or until warm. If you don't have a microwave, wrap the pancakes in a wet dish towel and warm in a 350°F oven for 8 to 10 minutes or until hot.

NOTE: It may be easier for you to simply buy pancakes at your local Chinese restaurant and reheat them.

Baby Shrimp with Cashews

MAKES APPROXIMATELY 3 CUPS.

- 4 tablespoons chicken broth
- 2 tablespoons soy sauce
- 2 tablespoons dry sherry
- 1 teaspoon cornstarch
- 1 teaspoon sugar
- 1 tablespoon sesame oil
- 4 scallions, finely sliced
- 1 pound raw baby shrimp, shelled, washed, and dried
- 1 cup roasted cashews

In a small bowl, combine the chicken broth, soy sauce, sherry, cornstarch, and sugar.

Heat a heavy skillet until very hot. Pour in sesame oil. When the oil is hot, add scallions and cook for 1 minute. Put the shrimp in the skillet and cook until pink, about 3 minutes. Pour in sauce. Cook until thick. Add the cashews and cook until hot, about 1 to 2 minutes. Spoon the filling into a Chinese pancake. Fold the pancake and serve.

Filled Chinese Pancakes.

87

Shredded Chicken in Peanut Sauce

MAKES 3 CUPS.

1 medium clove garlic
1 teaspoon fresh ginger slices
1/6 cup sesame oil
1/4 cup vegetable oil
1 tablespoon chili oil (optional)
1 tablespoon honey mustard
3 tablespoons rice vinegar
2 tablespoons soy sauce
4 tablespoons creamy peanut
   butter
Juice of 1 orange
3 cups cooked chicken,
   shredded
1/2 cucumber, julienned

Place the garlic, ginger, and oils in a blender or food processor fitted with the metal blade. Process until the garlic and ginger are pureed. Add the mustard, vinegar, soy sauce, and peanut butter. Process until all the ingredients are well blended. Pour in the orange juice and pulse until completely incorporated. Pour the peanut sauce over the chicken and toss until well combined.

Spoon the filling into a Chinese pancake. Garnish with cucumber. Fold the pancake and serve.

If you are making this filling in advance, refrigerate. Bring the filling back to room temperature before serving.

Sautéed Chinese Vegetables

MAKES APPROXIMATELY
2 1/2 TO 3 CUPS.

1 teaspoon plus 1 tablespoon
   sesame oil
1 egg, beaten
3 tablespoons chicken broth
3 tablespoons soy sauce
1 tablespoon sugar
1/2 teaspoon cornstarch
1 tablespoon vegetable oil
1 large clove garlic, minced
2 scallions, cut into 4-inch
   pieces and julienned
1 1/2 cups thinly sliced shiitake
   mushrooms
1 medium carrot, cut in half and
   julienned
1/2 cup fresh bean sprouts
1/2 cup bamboo shoots
1 cup thinly sliced Chinese
   cabbage
Plum or hoisin sauce

Heat 1 teaspoon sesame oil in a heavy skillet or wok until very hot.

Pour in beaten egg. Cook until firm. Turn over and cook for an additional minute. Remove to a plate and cut into very thin slices.

In a small bowl, combine chicken broth, soy sauce, sugar, and cornstarch. Set aside.

Heat 1 tablespoon each of sesame oil and vegetable oil in the skillet or wok until very hot.

Add garlic and cook for 30 seconds. Add the rest of the vegetables, sautéing for 5 minutes over high heat or until they start to lose their crunch.

Pour in reserved sauce and cook for an additional 3 minutes. Add egg, tossing well. Cook until egg is warmed. Spoon the filling onto a Chinese pancake. Top with plum or hoisin sauce. Fold the pancake and serve.

CRESCENT MOON MELON SLICES

MAKES 6 SLICES.

1/2 small honeydew melon
2 tablespoons plum wine,
   schnapps, or your favorite
   fruit liqueur

Remove all seeds and membrane from the melon half. Sprinkle the wine or liqueur over the melon. Cover with plastic wrap and refrigerate until chilled, 1 to 2 hours.

When ready to serve, cut the melon half into equal slices. Arrange on a plate. (If you have flowers, place a few in the center of the plate and arrange the melon slices around the flowers.)

Crescent Moon Melon Slices garnished with Sweet and Crunchy Walnuts and pineapple slices.

Decorated Almond Cakes.

ALMOND CAKES

MAKES APPROXIMATELY
1 DOZEN CAKES.

4 jumbo egg whites, at room
   temperature
1/2 cup superfine sugar
1 cup finely ground almonds
1 cup self-rising cake flour
2 teaspoons almond extract
12 blanched almonds
1/4 cup honey

Preheat oven to 325°F. Coat a 12-cup cup-cake tin with cooking spray.

In a large mixing bowl, beat the egg whites until they form soft peaks. Gradually add the sugar and continue beating until very stiff. Carefully fold in the ground almonds, then the flour, until both are completely incorporated. Gently mix in the almond extract.

Spoon the batter into the prepared cupcake tin. There should be enough batter to reach the rim of each cup. Place a blanched almond on top of each cup of batter. Bake for approximately 20 to 25 minutes or until the cakes are puffed, firm, and golden brown. Remove the tin from the oven and rest on a cooling rack.

Heat the honey in a microwave on high for 30 to 45 seconds or until hot and very fluid. (If you don't have a microwave, heat the honey in a small saucepan over low heat until hot.) Brush the honey lightly on the hot cakes. Let the cakes cool in the tin, then remove. The cakes are best served within 24 hours.

SWEET AND CRUNCHY WALNUTS

MAKES 1 CUP.

1 cup walnut halves
1 cup water
1/4 cup sugar
1/4 cup light Karo syrup
2 1/2 tablespoons unsalted butter

Place the walnuts in a small saucepan, cover with water, and bring to a boil. Boil for 1 minute. Remove from heat and drain off all water.

Pour the sugar and Karo syrup over walnuts. Stir well and return to the heat. Bring the mixture to a boil. Turn down heat and simmer for 10 minutes. One and a half minutes before the walnuts are ready, melt butter in a skillet and heat until hot.

Using a slotted spoon, remove walnuts from syrup, leaving as much syrup in the saucepan as possible. Add the walnuts to the butter and cook over medium-high heat until brown and crispy.

Using a slotted spoon, remove walnuts from the skillet, leaving as much of the drippings in the skillet as possible.

Spread the walnuts over a plate and let cool. If any excess caramelized sugar clings to the walnuts, simply break it off after they have cooled.

Stored in an airtight container, the walnuts should last at least a week.

NOTE: If after the walnuts have cooled you find them slightly greasy, lay them on a sheet of paper towel, cover with another sheet of paper towel, and pat gently.

CHAPTER TWELVE

CHILDREN'S TEA

Miniature Pita Pizzas

Peanut Butter and Jelly Sandwiches

Ham Sandwiches

Toll House Cookies

Cream Scones

Ice Cream Cone Cakes

Queen Mary (or your choice) Tea and Milk

Serves 6.

Oh, grown-ups cannot understand,
and grown-ups never will,
how short the way to fairyland
across the purple hill.
ALFRED NOYES

CHILDREN LOVE TEAS. THEY FIND MAGIC IN THEM AND ARE PREPARED TO be on their best behavior. Theirs is the remarkable ability to slip from the everyday and enter into the spirit of the occasion.

Children like having their sandwiches cut into small shapes and having the choices a Tea presents. The interesting thing about children at a Tea is that they only take as much as they can eat.

Naturally, we gear the Teas to suit their tastes, what children we know like, and what we liked as children. Pizzas and peanut butter and jelly sandwiches are standard favorites. The carrot and celery sticks are for the sake of mothers. As carrot and celery sticks are self-descriptive, we don't give a recipe. Do include the scones in your Tea. Children like them and will show you their thanks by politely trying them with both the cream and jam. The Toll House Cookies are such a favorite classic, nothing further need be said. The cone cakes were a fad in the 1950s. We had completely forgotten about them until a friend reminded us. The novelty alone entices children, and we remember being charmed. One additional tip if the children are drinking tea, substitute honey for sugar; they prefer it.

Keep in mind that it will make for a more comfortable Tea if you accommodate the china and seating arrangements to the children's size.

Finally, it's not necessary to have a special occasion for a children's Tea. Many of our friends do it once a week as a way of creating and sharing a special time with their children.

MINIATURE PITA PIZZAS

MAKES 6 PIZZAS.

- 6 tablespoons pizza sauce
- 6 1-ounce miniature pitas
- 1/2 cup grated mozzarella cheese
- 6 teaspoons grated parmesan cheese

Preheat broiler.

Spread 1 tablespoon of sauce on each pita. Sprinkle 4 teaspoons of mozzarella over the sauce on each pita. Sprinkle 1 teaspoon of parmesan cheese on each pita.

Using a spatula, place the pitas on an ungreased baking sheet. Place the baking sheet under the hot broiler and cook until the cheese is melted and crispy, approximately 3 to 5 minutes. Serve warm.

VARIATION: Most children prefer plain cheese pizza. If you wish, add additional toppings of your choice.

NOTE: Be careful not to put too much mozzarella on the pitas or the cheese will slide off.

Nutritious carrot and celery sticks.

PEANUT BUTTER AND JELLY SANDWICHES

MAKES 12 PIECES.

6 thin slices white bread
Unsalted butter
3 tablespoons creamy peanut
butter
3 tablespoons jelly or jam

Spread each slice of bread with a thin coating of butter.

Spread 1 tablespoon of peanut butter on each of 3 slices of bread. Spread 1 tablespoon of jelly on each of the remaining 3 slices of bread. Top the peanut butter slices with the jelly slices.

Trim the crusts. Cut each sandwich into 4 pieces.

NOTE: A fun idea for children is to use cookie cutters to cut out sandwiches that have different shapes or characters, such as stars and angels. Make the sandwiches first and then do the cutting. The thinness of the sandwich will adapt itself to cutting very easily.

One word of caution: Depending on the size of your cutters, you may have to adjust the number of sandwiches you make so that each child gets 2 pieces (if your cutters are large, 1 would do). Doing your sandwiches this way also increases probable waste, which may be a factor.

Ham Sandwiches

MAKES 12 PIECES.

6 thin slices wheat bread
Unsalted butter
3 slices boiled ham,
approximately 3 ounces
Mustard

Spread each slice of bread with a thin coating of butter. Lay a slice of ham on 3 slices of bread, folding the ham to conform to the size of the bread. Spread a smear of mustard on each slice of ham. Cover the bread with the remaining 3 slices. Trim the crusts. Cut each sandwich into 4 pieces.

NOTE: Please refer to note on page 95 (peanut-butter sandwiches) for directions on cutting the sandwiches into different shapes.

Toll House Cookies

MAKES 2¹/₂ DOZEN COOKIES.

1 cup plus 2 tablespoons
all-purpose flour
¹/₂ teaspoon baking soda
¹/₂ teaspoon salt
¹/₂ cup unsalted butter, softened
6 tablespoons sugar
6 tablespoons firmly packed
brown sugar
¹/₂ teaspoon vanilla extract
1 egg
1 6-ounce package (1 cup)
semisweet chocolate
morsels
¹/₂ cup chopped nuts

Preheat oven to 375°F.

In a small bowl, combine flour, baking soda, and salt. Set aside.

In a large bowl, combine butter, sugars, and vanilla extract.

Beat until creamy. Beat in egg. Gradually add flour mixture. Stir in chocolate morsels and nuts. Drop by rounded measuring tablespoons onto an ungreased cookie sheet.

Bake 9 to 11 minutes or until the cookies are brown on the edges. Cool and serve.

Cream Scones

MAKES APPROXIMATELY 10 SCONES.

2 cups flour
¹/₄ cup sugar
1 tablespoon baking powder
1 teaspoon salt
3 tablespoons unsalted butter,
cold
1 egg
1¹/₄ cups heavy cream
1 egg yolk
2 tablespoons cold water

Preheat oven to 350°F. Grease a baking sheet and set aside.

Sift the dry ingredients together. Using a pastry blender or 2 knives, cut in the butter until the mixture is crumbly.

Beat the egg and heavy cream together. Pour into the dry ingredients and stir until well blended.

Prepare a flat surface by flouring it well (the dough will be slightly wet and will absorb the flour quickly). Place the dough on the flat surface. Pat the dough down with your hands until it is ³/₄-inch thick. Cut out the scones with a 2¹/₂-inch biscuit cutter and place on a greased baking sheet.

Beat the egg yolk with the cold water. Using a pastry brush, glaze scones with this mixture.

Bake for 25 to 30 minutes or until golden brown.

Serve hot or cold with jam and Clotted Cream, if desired.

Cream Scones with Clotted Cream and jam.

ICE CREAM CONE CAKES

MAKES 6 CONES.

6 Nabisco™ Comet cones
1½ cups Grandma Paradis'
     Quickie Chocolate Cake
     batter
1 cup Easy Yellow Cake batter
Buttercream Frosting
3 maraschino cherries
Sprinkles

Preheat oven to 350°F.

Place the 6 empty cones upright in a cupcake tin.

Fill 3 cones with ½ cup each of the chocolate cake batter, then fill the remaining cones with ⅓ cup each of the yellow cake batter.

Place the muffin tin carefully in the oven and bake for 25 to 30 minutes or until the cake has puffed up firm and golden brown. Remove from oven and cool.

Frost the top of each cone cake with 2 tablespoons of Buttercream Frosting, swirling the knife (or spoon) as you go. Cut the cherries in half and place on top, cut-side down. Cover generously with sprinkles.

Grandma Paradis' Quickie Chocolate Cake

MAKES 1 THIN 9-INCH LAYER OR
2½ CUPS BATTER.

¾ cup sugar
1 egg
2 tablespoons shortening
    (such as Crisco)
1 teaspoon baking soda
    dissolved in ½ cup
    buttermilk
½ teaspoon salt
1 cup all-purpose flour
1½ teaspoons vanilla
¼ cup unsweetened cocoa
    dissolved in ¼ cup boiling
    water
Confectioner's sugar

Preheat oven to 350°F. Grease a 9-inch cake pan and set aside.

Mix all ingredients except the cocoa and confectioner's sugar in a bowl. Beat for 1 minute.

Add the cocoa and beat for 2 minutes or until batter is smooth. Pour batter into cake pan.

Bake for 30 to 35 minutes or until cake is firm and springs back to the touch. Cool in pan. Remove to a plate and dust with confectioner's sugar.

NOTE: If using this recipe for the Ice Cream Cone Cakes, do *not* bake the batter until it has been poured into the cones.

Easy Yellow Cake

MAKES 2 9-INCH LAYERS OR
4 CUPS BATTER.

½ cup shortening (such as
     Crisco), at room
     temperature
1 cup sugar
2 eggs
2 cups all-purpose flour
½ teaspoon salt
2 teaspoons baking powder
1 cup milk
½ teaspoon vanilla

Preheat oven to 350°F. Grease 2 9-inch cake pans and set aside.

Cream the shortening. Gradually add the sugar and continue to cream. Add the eggs, 1 at a time, beating after each addition.

Sift the dry ingredients together. Add the dry ingredients (⅓ at a time) alternating with the milk, to the creamed mixture. Beat until smooth. Pour in vanilla and mix well. Divide batter between the 2 cake pans.

Bake for 30 to 35 minutes or until cake is golden and springs back to the touch.

NOTE: If using this recipe for the Ice Cream Cone Cakes, do *not* bake the batter until it has been poured into the cones.

Brightly decorated Ice Cream Cone Cakes.

Buttercream Frosting

MAKES 1¹/₃ CUPS, ENOUGH TO FROST
6 CONES.

- 6 **tablespoons butter, softened**
- 2 **cups confectioner's sugar**
- 1 **teaspoon vanilla**
- 2 **tablespoons hot milk**

Cream the butter and sugar until smooth. Mix in the vanilla. Beat in the hot milk until the frosting is creamy. Place in the refrigerator so that the frosting becomes firm and spreadable.

This frosting is best when made close to frosting time.

NOTE: The cake part of dessert can be baked the day before, wrapped in wax paper or plastic wrap. Use any leftover cake batter to make cupcakes.

CHAPTER THIRTEEN

CHOCOLATE LOVER'S TEA

Prosciutto and Explorateur Cheese Sandwiches

Smoked Turkey and Chutney Sandwiches

Sliced Chicken Sandwiches

Chocolate Dipped Shortbread Hearts

Chocolate-Chip Scones

Chocolate Delight Cake

White Chocolate Dipped Fruit

Chocolate Truffles

Irish Breakfast Tea (or your choice)

Serves 6.

CHOCOLATE HAS BEEN CALLED A GIFT FROM THE GODS, THE BEDTIME companion of choice, and the perfect meal. It was used by the Aztecs as both medicine and aphrodisiac. Some scientists believe that eating chocolate triggers a release in the brain of the same chemical that is released when we are in love. Athletes use it as a source of energy and husbands and lovers use it as the perfect Valentine's Day gift. There are a lot of reasons to eat chocolate. But who needs a reason? Its creamy deliciousness has always been reason enough.

Not everyone is a chocolate devotee. Some, a minority, no doubt, have little or no use for it. If that is the case, then this Tea is not for them. It is for those who glory and revel in the dark delight; those who appreciate an afternoon of unrestrained pleasure.

This is a rich Tea and it is absolutely meant to be so. It is not one you would have every week or even every month. Rather, it suits a very special occasion when you and your guests have decided to forget about calories and simply enjoy yourselves.

For variety we have added a touch of spice to the sandwiches. We like the way spicy foods and chocolate play off one another.

Serve clotted cream with this Tea just as with every other. Some hardy guests have even been known to have a spoon of it with their cake, so you might consider making extra.

Have fun with this. Use some of your own chocolate favorites if you wish, and give in to an afternoon of sybaritic pleasure.

PROSCIUTTO AND EXPLORATEUR CHEESE SANDWICHES

MAKES 12 PIECES.

6 thin slices white bread
Unsalted butter
3 ounces Explorateur cheese,
    at room temperature
2 ounces thinly sliced
    prosciutto, approximately

Spread each slice of bread with a thin coating of butter.

Spread a thin layer of cheese on 3 slices of bread. Lay a slice of prosciutto on the cheese, folding the prosciutto to conform to the size of the bread. Cover the 3 sandwiches with the remaining bread.

Trim the crusts. Cut each sandwich into 4 pieces.

SMOKED TURKEY AND CHUTNEY SANDWICHES

MAKES 12 PIECES.

6 thin slices wheat bread
Unsalted butter
3 slices smoked turkey,
    approximately 3 ounces
    total
3 teaspoons chutney of your
    choice (we use mango)

Spread each slice of bread with a thin coating of butter. Lay a slice of turkey on 3 slices of bread. Spread a teaspoon of chutney on each slice of turkey. Top the bread with the remaining slices. Trim the crusts. Cut each sandwich into 4 pieces.

SLICED CHICKEN SANDWICHES

MAKES 12 PIECES.

6 thin slices white bread
Unsalted butter
6 ounces cooked chicken breast,
    thinly sliced
Salt (to taste)
Pepper (to taste)

Spread each slice of bread with a thin coating of butter. Divide the chicken slices (2 ounces per sandwich) between 3 pieces of bread. Salt and pepper each sandwich. Cover each sandwich with the remaining bread. Trim the crusts. Cut each sandwich into 4 pieces.

CHOCOLATE DIPPED SHORTBREAD HEARTS

MAKES APPROXIMATELY
4 DOZEN COOKIES.

1 **pound unsalted butter**
1 **cup sugar**
4 **cups flour**
8 **ounces semisweet chocolate**

Preheat oven to 375°F.

Cream butter. Add sugar gradually. Add flour, making sure it is well mixed, but don't overwork. Pat out the dough on a lightly floured board until it is about ³/₄-inch thick. Using a 2-inch heart-shaped cookie cutter, cut out hearts and place on an ungreased cookie sheet. Cook 15 to 20 minutes or until cookies are golden brown on the edges. Watch the first few batches closely and lower oven to 350°F or 325°F if they cook too quickly.

Place baked cookies on a rack to cool. Melt the chocolate in a microwave-proof container for about 45 seconds per square, depending on the oven. (If you don't have a microwave oven, melt the chocolate in the top of a double boiler that has been coated with cooking spray until the chocolate liquidizes.) Dip half the heart into the melted chocolate so that you have a black and white effect.

Lay dipped hearts on a plate covered with wax paper. Place plate in the refrigerator 1 hour or until chocolate has set.

Store the hearts in a cool, dry container with sheets of wax paper between the layers. Undipped hearts can be frozen up to 2 months, providing they are well wrapped.

Chocolate Dipped Shortbread Hearts garnished with flowers.

CHOCOLATE CHIP SCONES

MAKES APPROXIMATELY 10 SCONES.

2 **cups flour**
¹/₄ **cup sugar**
2 **teaspoons baking powder**
1 **teaspoon salt**
3 **tablespoons unsalted butter**
1 **egg**
³/₄ **cup milk**
¹/₂ **cup chocolate morsels**
1 **egg yolk**
2 **tablespoons cold water**

Preheat oven to 350°F.

Sift the dry ingredients together. Using a pastry blender or 2 knives, cut in the butter until crumbly.

Beat the egg and milk together. Pour into the dry ingredients, stirring until a dough is formed. Add the chocolate chips, combining well.

Using an ice cream scoop, form the scones and place on a greased baking sheet.

Beat the egg yolk with the cold water. Using a pastry brush, glaze each scone with this mixture.

Bake for 25 to 30 minutes or until golden brown.

Serve hot or cold with jam and Clotted Cream, if desired.

Chocolate Delight Cake garnished with flowers.

CHOCOLATE DELIGHT CAKE

A DARK, RICH CAKE WITH AN EVEN darker, richer frosting. This cake is a chocolate lover's delight.

MAKES 1 10-INCH TUBE CAKE.

Dark Chocolate Cake

- 4 ounces unsweetened chocolate
- 1 tablespoon instant coffee granules
- 2 cups cake flour
- 2 teaspoons baking soda
- ½ teaspoon salt
- ½ pound butter, at room temperature
- 1½ cups packed dark brown sugar
- 3 eggs, at room temperature
- 2 teaspoons vanilla
- ½ cup buttermilk
- ½ cup boiling water

Preheat oven to 350°F. Grease a 10-inch tube cake pan and set aside.

Melt the chocolate and coffee together in the top half of a double boiler or microwave. Cool to room temperature.

Combine the flour, baking soda, and salt. In a large bowl, cream the butter and sugar. Add the eggs to the butter and sugar mixture 1 at a time, beating until well mixed. Pour in the vanilla, beating an additional 30 seconds. Add the cooled chocolate and coffee and beat until well blended.

Spoon in one-third of the flour mixture and ¼ cup of buttermilk, beating until mixed. Repeat.

Add the last of the flour, blending well. Beat in the boiling water until it is fully absorbed and incorporated in the batter. Pour the batter into the prepared cake pan. Bake for 45 minutes to 1 hour or until a toothpick inserted in the center comes out clean.

Let sit in the pan for 10 minutes, then turn out onto a serving plate or platter. Cool completely.

Chocolate Ganache

MAKES APPROXIMATELY 3/4 CUP, ENOUGH TO FROST 1 10-INCH CAKE.

6 ounces semisweet chocolate
1/2 cup heavy cream

Break the chocolate into small bits. (You can put it in a food processor fitted with the metal blade and process until it is very finely chopped.) Put the chocolate into a medium-size bowl.

Heat the cream to boiling point. Whisk the hot cream into the chocolate and continue whisking until the chocolate is melted and blended with the cream.

Let sit, covered, until it reaches room temperature.

NOTE: This frosting can sit out on your counter, covered, overnight, and still be good for use. Do not refrigerate, for it will become hard.

To frost the cake, spoon 1/4 cup of the Chocolate Ganache around the top of the cake, letting it drip down the sides.

Using a knife, spread the ganache so that the entire cake has a very thin coating.

Put cake in the refrigerator and chill until the ganache starts to set, approximately 45 minutes. Remove from refrigerator and frost with the remaining ganache until the cake is coated with a thick, even layer.

Chill until set, approximately 1 1/2 hours. This cake is best served at room temperature.

Just before serving, decorate the top of the cake with small, fresh flowers or the decorations of your choice.

WHITE CHOCOLATE DIPPED FRUIT

MAKES APPROXIMATELY 12 PIECES OF FRUIT.

7 ounces white chocolate for dipping
6 large navel orange sections, excess pith and membrane removed
6 large strawberries, washed and dried

Melt the white chocolate in the top half of a double boiler. Holding the orange sections at the top, dip each slice into the chocolate until two-thirds of the slice is covered. Place the fruit on a wax paper-covered plate.

Gently holding the hull, dip the strawberries into the chocolate until two-thirds of each strawberry is covered. Place the strawberries on the plate.

Refrigerate the fruit until the chocolate is set, approximately 1/2 to 1 hour. These should be made on the day of the Tea.

CHOCOLATE TRUFFLES

MAKES APPROXIMATELY 2 DOZEN TRUFFLES.

8 ounces semisweet chocolate
3/4 cup heavy cream
1 1/2 tablespoons rum (optional)
Powdered cocoa
Paper bonbon cups

Place the chocolate in a food processor fitted with the metal blade, or break by hand. Pulse until finely grated and transfer to a bowl.

In a saucepan, heat the heavy cream until it scalds. Pour the hot cream over the chocolate and whisk the mixture together until the chocolate is melted and both are well blended. Add the rum, if desired.

Cover the mixture and refrigerate until it has cooled and thickened, approximately 3 to 4 hours.

Using a teaspoon, place a mound of dough in the palm of your hand. Roll it into a ball, then roll in powdered cocoa until it is completely covered. Place the truffle in a bonbon cup.

NOTE: If you find it difficult to shape the truffles, add 2 tablespoons of soft butter to the mix and refrigerate until it is set.

CHAPTER FOURTEEN

FEEL BETTER TEA

Chicken Consummé

Hot Buttered Toast

Red Egg on Toast°

Fruit Sherbet

Herbal Tea

Serves 6.

W HAVE ALL SUFFERED FROM A COLD OR FLU THAT HAS MADE US FEEL as though we were at death's door. We lay on our bed feeling miserable. Then, the door would open and someone would come in bringing hot soup or tea. They would put their hand on our forehead. We'd feel a little better. The room didn't seem as dark. It's amazing how a little care and attention helps to heal.

We never can remember if it's feed a cold and starve a fever, or vice versa. Perhaps the "patient" really isn't up to having anything, but the caring a simple tea tray represents will help lift the spirits. The food *will* help. A good broth provides nourishment and the toast provides easy sustenance. The tea and sherbert soothe the throat while giving the body needed liquid.

Remember to make the tray look as appealing as possible. Put a nice cloth on it, a flower in a vase, and use a china cup for the tea. This will help both body and spirit.

Hot Buttered Toast, tea, and jam.

HOT BUTTERED TOAST

MAKES 8 PIECES.

❁

Unsalted butter
2 slices bread

Toast the bread. Butter it lightly. Trim the crusts. Cut each slice into 4 diagonal pieces (called toast points). Serve warm.

RED EGG ON TOAST

SERVES 1.

❁

Red Egg on Toast may be served to the patient when the "crisis" has passed and something more is required. This childhood favorite is a tasty, filling, and gentle form of nourishment.

Unsalted butter
1 egg
1 slice bread
¹/₄ cup canned tomato soup,
      undiluted

Put a teaspoon of butter in a small skillet and heat on low heat until melted. Gently crack an egg into the butter and cook for 1 minute on each side.

While the egg is cooking, toast and butter a slice of bread. Place on a plate. Put the egg on the toast.

Heat the soup until hot, either in the microwave (1 minute on high) or on the top of the stove. Spoon the hot soup over the egg, making sure to cover the egg and toast entirely. Serve hot.

CHICKEN CONSOMMÉ

MAKES APPROXIMATELY 1½ CUPS.

4 large chicken legs
   (approximately
   2½ pounds)
1 carrot, cut into 4 pieces
1 celery stalk, cut into 4 pieces
1 large clove garlic, cut into
   4 pieces
1 medium onion, cut into
   8 sections
1 teaspoon parsley
½ teaspoon rosemary
½ teaspoon basil
2 quarts cold water
Salt (to taste)

Put the chicken, carrot, celery, garlic, and onion in a large pot. Place the herbs in the center of a 2-inch square piece of cheesecloth. Bring the corners together, creating a pouch, and twist. Tie with string to secure. Add the bag to the pot. Pour in the cold water.

Bring the mixture to a boil, then lower heat and simmer for 2 hours. Remove the cheesecloth pouch.

Pour the entire mixture through a strainer to separate the chicken and vegetables from the broth. Return the broth to the pot. Skim off and remove any apparent fat. Cook the broth on medium-high heat until reduced by half. Season lightly with salt and serve.

The consommé can be safely kept in the refrigerator for 1 week, and freezes well for at least 3 months. Once it is thawed, use within 24 hours.

Chicken Consommé, Hot Buttered Toast, and Herb Tea.

CHAPTER FIFTEEN

LATE-NIGHT TEA

California Chicken Sandwiches

Maggie Barry's Half-Pound Poppy Seed Cake

Cream of Tomato Soup

Fresh Sliced Fruit

Earl Grey Tea (or your choice)

Serves 2.

Wᴇ'ᴠᴇ ᴅᴇsɪɢɴᴇᴅ ᴛʜɪs Tᴇᴀ ꜰᴏʀ ᴛʜᴏsᴇ ᴇᴠᴇɴɪɴɢs ᴡʜᴇɴ ʏᴏᴜ ᴀʀᴇ ᴏᴜᴛ ʟᴀᴛᴇ but want to create a nice meal at home with a minimum of fuss.

Both the Cream of Tomato Soup and Poppy Seed Cake can be made a day or two in advance. Slice the chicken, mix the alfalfa sprouts with the mayonnaise, and sprinkle the peeled, sliced avocado with lemon. Put them all (covered well) in the refrigerator until you need them. Wash and dry the fruit, if necessary. When you come home, assemble the sandwiches, heat the soup, and slice the fruit and cake. You're ready to serve.

A Tea such as this provides a wonderful opportunity for a dinner à deux. Take advantage of this opportunity and create a romantic setting. Set the table before leaving with freshly pressed linen, your nicest dishes, long-stemmed glasses for water (or wine), and candles. Buy fresh flowers and arrange them in a small vase, nothing too large, because you want to keep the setting intimate. setting intimate.

Enjoy your evening out. You'll be coming home knowing the best of it lies ahead.

California Chicken Sandwiches

MAKES 2 OPEN-FACED SANDWICHES.

2 **thick slices pumpernickel bread**
1 **cup alfalfa sprouts**
1/3 **cup mayonnaise**
1/2 **small avocado**
1 **teaspoon fresh lemon or lime juice**
6 **ounces cooked chicken, thinly sliced**
2 **ounces Swiss or Jarlsberg cheese**
1/2 **teaspoon sesame seeds**

Toast 1 side of the bread under a hot broiler.

Mix together the alfalfa sprouts and mayonnaise, blending well. Cut the avocado into 8 thin slices. Sprinkle the citrus juice over the avocado slices. Spread one-half of the sprouts and mayonnaise mixture on the untoasted side of each slice of bread.

Place 4 avocado slices on top of the sprouts. Divide the chicken slices between the 2 sandwiches, placing them on top of the avocado. Place 1 ounce of sliced cheese over the top of each sandwich. Sprinkle 1/4 teaspoon sesame seeds over each sandwich.

Using a spatula, put the sandwiches on a baking sheet and broil until the cheese is melted and starting to puff and brown, about 5 to 10 minutes. Serve immediately.

Maggie Barry's Half-Pound Poppy Seed Cake

MAKES 1 9-BY-5-BY-3-INCH LOAF.

1/2 **pound unsalted butter, at room temperature**
1 **cup sugar**
2 **eggs, at room temperature**
2 **teaspoons vanilla**
2 **cups self-rising cake flour**
1/2 **cup milk**
3 **tablespoons poppy seeds**

Preheat oven to 350°F. Grease a 9-by-5-by-3-inch loaf pan and set aside.

Cream the butter in a mixer until light and fluffy, about 1 minute. Pour in sugar and repeat process. Add the eggs and vanilla and beat for an additional 30 seconds. Add the flour, 1 cup at a time, beating until combined. Pour in the milk and beat until smooth. Add poppy seeds and blend. Pour batter into the prepared loaf pan, pressing down with a spoon to remove air pockets.

Bake for 45 minutes to 1 hour, or until golden brown and a toothpick inserted in the center comes out clean. Remove from oven and cool on a cake rack. When the pan is cool, remove the cake from the pan and let it sit on the cake rack until it is completely cool.

Serve plain or lightly toasted with butter and preserves.

Well wrapped, the cake will last 5 days.

California Chicken Sandwiches and Earl Grey Tea.

Cream of Tomato Soup served with Crackers.

CREAM OF TOMATO SOUP

MAKES APPROXIMATELY 4½ CUPS.

4 tablespoons plus 2 teaspoons
  unsalted butter
1 medium yellow onion,
  coarsely chopped
14 plum tomatoes (3 cups),
  peeled, seeded, and cut
  into quarters
2 cups chicken broth
½ cup heavy cream
  Salt (to taste)

Melt 4 tablespoons of the butter in a large saucepan over medium-high heat until it just starts to brown. Add the onion and cook until translucent and starting to brown, about 2 minutes. Put in the tomatoes and cook until soft, about 3 minutes. Pour in the chicken broth and bring to a boil. Turn the heat down and simmer for 5 minutes.

Purée the soup in a food processor fitted with the metal blade or a blender. Return the soup to the pot and bring to a boil.

Add the heavy cream and 2 teaspoons butter, continuing to heat until the butter is melted and soup is hot. Season with salt.

This soup will stay fresh in the refrigerator 3 to 5 days; it can be frozen for up to 6 months.

FRESH SLICED FRUIT

SERVES 2.

DEPENDING ON THE SEASON, WE SUGGEST you choose one of the combinations listed below.

½ **small honeydew melon**
1 **pint strawberries**
or
1 **fresh Bosc pear**
1 **ripe kiwi**

Melon and Strawberries:
    Early in the day of your Tea, wash and dry the strawberries. Seed the half melon and cut into 4 slices. Arrange the 4 slices of melon around the edge of a plate so it makes a circle. Place the strawberries in the middle of the plate. Cover with plastic wrap and refrigerate until needed.

Pear and Kiwi:
    Just before serving, peel and cut the kiwi into ¼-inch slices. Lay them, overlapping, in a circular pattern in the center of a plate. Cut the pear into 8 slices and cut out the center core. Lay the pear slices evenly around the plate, extending outward from the kiwi circle to create a sunburst effect.

Fresh Sliced Fruit and Maggie Barry's Half Pound Poppy Seed Cake (see recipe on page 112).

CHAPTER SIXTEEN

BARE BONES TEA

Any Combination of:

Grilled Cheese Sandwiches

"Whatever" Croques

Creamed Mushrooms

Easy Crepes

Peanut Butter and Banana Sandwiches

Cinnamon Toast Fingers

Herb Omelet

Toast Points with Jam

Black Currant Tea (or your choice)

Serves 2.

W̶E ALL HAVE HAD THOSE TIMES WHEN SOMEONE DROPS BY UNEXPECT-edly. We are glad to see the guest and would like to make an "occasion" of the visit, but the cupboards seem bare. What to do?

We can help. The following suggestions and recipes can be made with a minimum of fuss and waste. These simple ideas will keep you prepared for any of those times when you would like to do a little something extra. Any one of the recipes given is sufficient to provide a small Tea we call "bare bones."

Always keep some nice cookies in your cupboard. Packaged cookies generally have a long shelf life. Be sure to carefully close opened packages to ensure that the remaining cookies don't go stale. Arrange the cookies on a small plate and serve with tea.

Bake one of the pound cakes named in earlier chapters (see pages 41, 104, and 112) and store in the freezer. When you have a need for the cake, slice off what you need and return the remainder to the freezer. To thaw, let the cake sit for 10 to 15 minutes covered in plastic wrap. You can speed up the process by heating the covered cake in a microwave for approximately 15 seconds on high. A nice touch would be to toast the pound cake, butter it, and cut it into finger-size pieces.

Bake the shortbread hearts (see page 103), omitting the chocolate dipping, or any of the cookies from previous chapters, and keep them in the freezer. Take them out as needed. A short time at room temperature will quickly render them edible.

Toast Points with Jam

MAKES 8 PIECES.

**Jam
2 thin slices white bread
Unsalted butter**

Fill a small bowl with jam. Set the bowl in the middle of a plate.

Toast the bread and butter it well. Trim the crusts. Cut each slice into 4 diagonal pieces. Arrange the 8 toast points around the bowl of jam.

Creamed Mushrooms

MAKES 1 CUP.

CREAMED MUSHROOMS ARE A TASTY tidbit and easy to prepare. Keeping a small can of sliced mushrooms in the cupboard is no bother—and will always come in handy.

**1 3-ounce can sliced mushrooms
1 tablespoon butter or
   margarine
4 teaspoons flour
1/2 cup milk
Pinch nutmeg
Salt (to taste)
Pepper (to taste)**

Open and drain the can of mushrooms, reserving the liquid (approximately three-eighths of a can).

Heat a small skillet over medium-low heat. Add the butter and melt until foamy. Whisk in the flour, beating until the roux is smooth. Let the roux cook until it starts to brown, approximately 1 to 2 minutes. Whisk in the reserved mushroom juice.

As the sauce starts to thicken, add the milk and beat until smooth. Spoon in the sliced mushrooms and heat until the mushrooms are hot. Add a generous pinch of nutmeg (not too much or the sauce will be bitter), and season with salt and pepper.

Serve the mushrooms hot over toast points (see page 108).

GRILLED CHEESE SANDWICHES

MAKES 8 PIECES.

KEEP BREAD AND CHEDDAR CHEESE IN the freezer and use it to make grilled sandwiches.

Unsalted butter
4 slices bread
1 cup grated cheese (just take it from the freezer and grate it)
1/8 teaspoon basil (or herb of your choice)

Coat a skillet with cooking spray. Generously butter 2 slices of bread. Lay them butter side down on the skillet.

Carefully place 1/2 cup of grated cheese on each sandwich. Sprinkle a small amount of herbs (fresh are best) on the cheese.

Butter the remaining bread slices and place on top of the grated cheese, butter side up.

Turn the flame to low. Cook the sandwiches for 3 minutes on each side or until they are golden brown. Cover the pan with a lid and let cook for an additional 2 minutes to ensure the cheese is melted.

Place on plates and cut each sandwich into 4 pieces. Serve hot.

Assorted cookies, pound cake, and tea.

119

Cinnamon toast can be served whole or cut into fingers.

CINNAMON TOAST FINGERS

MAKES 8 PIECES.

 2 slices bread, preferably sliced
    thick
 2 teaspoons sugar
 ¹/₂ teaspoon cinnamon
    Unsalted butter

Toast 1 side of the 2 bread slices under a broiler or in a toaster oven. In a small bowl, combine the sugar and cinnamon.

Generously butter the untoasted sides of bread. Divide the sugar and cinnamon between the 2 toasts, sprinkling evenly over the entire surface. Return the bread to the broiler and cook until the sugar is bubbling, about 5 minutes. Remove the toast from the oven and cut each slice into 4 fingers.

NOTE: For a nice touch, take a pretty piece of linen or embroidered cloth, lay it on a small plate, pile the toast fingers on it, and bring up the corners to cover the toast and serve.

"WHATEVER" CROQUES

MAKES 8 PIECES.

YOU CAN PUT TOGETHER A CROQUE-TYPE sandwich using any bits and pieces you have in the refrigerator.

    Unsalted butter
 4 slices bread
 2 ounces (2 slices) whatever
    luncheon type meat you
    have available (leftover
    chicken or turkey
    work, too)
 2 ounces (2 slices) whatever
    cheese you have in the
    refrigerator or freezer
 2 eggs, beaten
 2 tablespoons milk
 2 tablespoons butter or
    margarine (for grilling)

Butter the 4 slices of bread. Place 1 ounce of meat and 1 ounce of cheese on 2 of the slices of bread. Top the sandwiches with the remaining bread. Set aside.

In a bowl or baking dish, mix the beaten eggs with the milk. Holding the sandwiches tightly, lay them in the egg batter.

Turn the sandwiches so that they are completely covered with egg. Let them sit in the batter while you prepare the skillet, turning them every 30 seconds or so.

Put 2 tablespoons of butter into a medium-size skillet and heat over medium-low flame. When the butter is hot and foamy, carefully lay the sandwiches in the skillet. Cook until golden brown on 1 side, about 3 to 5 minutes. Repeat on the other side.

Turn the heat down very low, cover the pan, and cook the sandwiches 1 additional minute to ensure the cheese is melted.

Place the sandwiches on plates and cut into 4 pieces. Serve hot.

EASY CREPES

MAKES APPROXIMATELY 6 CREPES.

¹/₂ cup all-purpose flour
1 tablespoon sugar
¹/₈ teaspoon salt
1 egg
¹/₂ cup milk
1 tablespoon melted butter or margarine, at room temperature
Vegetable oil
Butter or margarine (for spreading)
Granulated or confectioner's sugar
Preserves

In a small bowl, combine the flour, sugar, and salt. In a separate bowl beat the egg with the milk. Whisk the egg mixture into the flour mixture, beating until smooth. Pour in the melted butter and mix well until blended.

Coat a small skillet with a cooking spray. Heat the skillet over a low flame until hot, then lightly brush it with vegetable oil. It should not be necessary to repeat this process, but if the crepes start to stick, do so as necessary.

Pour 2¹/₂ tablespoons of batter into the skillet, moving the skillet in a circular motion to spread the batter in a circle that covers the bottom of the pan.

Cook for approximately 30 seconds or until lightly browned. Turn over and cook until lightly browned, approximately 30 seconds. Remove crepe from pan. Spread lightly with butter. Roll up and keep in a warm oven while you cook the rest.

When all the crepes are cooked, place them on a warm plate. Sprinkle confectioner's or granulated sugar over the top and serve.

Your favorite fruit preserve is a lovely accompaniment to the crepes.

HERB OMELET

MAKES 2 SMALL OMELETS.

4 large eggs
4 tablespoons cold water
2 teaspoons dried herb of your choice (or 1 teaspoon fresh)
3 teaspoons butter

Break 2 eggs into a glass. Add 2 tablespoons cold water and 1 teaspoon herbs. Put 1¹/₂ teaspoons butter into a small skillet and heat on medium-low until the butter is melted and hot.

While the butter is melting, beat the eggs with a fork. (Using a glass limits the amount of air that goes into the eggs, giving you a fluffier omelet.)

Pour the egg into the hot butter and cook, covered, until the top of the omelet is done. Slide the omelet onto a plate, folding it in half as you do. Keep the omelet in a warm oven while you repeat this process for the second omelet.

Serve hot with toast points (see page 108).

PEANUT BUTTER AND BANANA SANDWICHES

MAKES 8 PIECES.

PEANUT BUTTER HAS BEEN AN AMERICAN favorite ever since George Washington Carver invented it, and it is now a staple in most homes. Combine it with banana and you get a nutritious snack that is easy to produce on the spur of the moment.

Butter
4 slices bread
4 tablespoons peanut butter
¹/₂ ripe banana

Spread each slice of bread with a thin coating of butter.

Evenly spread 2 tablespoons of peanut butter on 2 of the slices of bread. Cut the banana into thin slices and lay the slices on top of the peanut butter, dividing evenly. Top the sandwiches with the remaining bread.

Trim the crusts. Cut each sandwich into 4 pieces.

SOURCES

The following organizations and companies were very helpful in providing us with tea information.

BENCHLEY TEA
RD #1 178-G
Highway 34 and Ridgewood Road
Wall Township, New Jersey 07719

R. C. BIGELOW, INC.
15 Merwin Street
Norwalk, Connecticut 06856

CADBURY TYPHOO LTD
Franklin House
P.O. Box 171
Bounville, Birmingham B30 2NA
England

CELESTIAL SEASONINGS (Herbal Teas)
1780 55th Street
Boulder, Colorado 80301-2795

JACKSONS OF PICCADILLY
66–72 St. Johns Road
Clapham Junctions
London SW11 1PT
England

THOMAS J. LIPTON, INC.
800 Sylvan Avenue
Englewood Cliffs, New Jersey 07632

LYONS TETLEY LTD
325 Old Field Lande
Greenford, Middlesex UB6 0A82
England

TEA ASSOCIATION OF THE U.S.A.
230 Park Avenue
New York, New York 10169

TEA & COFFEE ASSOCIATION OF CANADA
1185 Eglinton Avenue East
Suite 101
Don Mills, Ontario
M3C 3C6

TEA COUNCIL OF CANADA
Suite 501
701 Evans Avenue
Etobicoke, Ontario
M9C 1A3

TEA COUNCIL OF THE U.S.A.
230 Park Avenue
New York, New York 10169

Photographer/KATRINA DELEON
Prop and Set Stylies/JANE PANICO-TRZECIAK
Food Stylist/MARIANNE S. TWOHIE
Special thanks for set construction/MARTIN
DELEON

CHAPTER 1 / TEA THE DRINK

Metal tea canister
PANTRY AND HEARTH
121 East 35th Street
New York, NY 10016

CHAPTER 3 / A BRITISH CREAM TEA

*Silver tea set, biscuit box (Scones) pastry/sandwich
stand, silver tray (Tarts), and server*
MICHAEL FEINBERG
225 5th Avenue
New York, NY 10001

Crystal vase
MILLER ROGASKA
225 5th Avenue
New York, NY 10001

Napkins
WOLFMAN-GOLD & GOOD CO.
116 Greene St
New York, NY 10012

Cake stand (Sponge Cake), tea cups and saucers
BARDITH
31 E 72nd Street
New York, NY 10021

CHAPTER 4 / AN AMERICAN CREAM TEA

Cups and saucers
L/S COLLECTION
225 5th Avenue
New York, NY 10001

*Cake stand (Lemon Bundt Cake), tart plate, sandwich
plate, napkin, napkin ring, and silver tea set*
EUROMART
1-800-356-6870

CHAPTER 5 / A SOUTHERN TEA

Location
Rocky Pines
Eldred, NY 12732

Wicker table and chair
WICKERY
342 3rd Avenue
New York, NY 10010

*Pedestal cake plate (Coconut Cake), pedestal compote
(Scones), tart plate, ceramic platter, sandwich and
cookie plate, tea pots and teacups*
PORTA
225 5th Avenue
New York, NY 10001

Napkins, cake server, and ice tea glasses
WOLFMAN-GOLD & GOOD CO.
116 Greene Street
New York, NY 10012

Glass pitcher
MILLER ROGASKA
225 5th Avenue
New York, NY 10001

CHAPTER 6 / HIGH TEA

Tea set, cups, fruit bowl, glass bowl (Chutney)
BARDITH
31 East 72nd Street
New York, NY 10021

CHAPTER 7 / THANKSGIVING TEA

Chair, napkins, and metal box
PANTRY AND HEARTH
121 East 35th Street
New York, NY 10016

CHAPTER 8 / CHRISTMAS TEA

Tea set, cups, tiered sandwich plate, and small bowl
GALLERY 726
225 5th Avenue
New York, NY 10001

*Silver basket, and napkin (Scones), gold candlesticks,
cookie plate, and small bowl*
GALLERY 320
225 5th Avenue
New York, NY 10001

Napkin
WOLFMAN-GOLD & GOOD CO.
116 Greene Street
New York, NY 10012

CHAPTER 9 / EASTER TEA

Napkin rings and cake plate
FITZ AND FLOYD
225 5th Avenue
New York, NY 10001

Sandwich plate (Catalina pattern)
VILLEROY AND BACH
225 5th Avenue
New York, NY 10001

Teapot, Stand, cups, saucers, ceramic rabbit, and ceramic basket
H. LEXINGTON COLLECTION
907 Madison Avenue
New York, NY 10021

Ceramic easter eggs
ARTORIA/PORCELAIN DE LIMOGES
225 Fifth Avenue
New York, NY 10001

Napkin inside ceramic basket
DEBORAH MALLOW DESIGNS, INC.
1261 Broadway, Suite 1010
New York, NY 10001

Catalina pattern plate (Strawberries and Lemon Crisps)
VILLEROY AND BACH
225 5th Avenue
New York, NY 10001

CHAPTER 10 / RUSSIAN TEA

Tablecloth and Napkins
DEBORAH MALLOW DESIGNS, INC.
1261 Broadway, Suite 1010
New York, NY 10001

CHAPTER 11 / CHINESE TEA

Tea pot and cups
TERRI SHAPIRO, artist

Placemats, napkins, and basket
POTTERY BARN
700 Broadway
New York, NY 10003

Chopsticks, chopstick Stands, and fan
FIVE EGGS
436 West Broadway
New York, NY 10012

CHAPTER 12 / CHILDREN'S TEA

Tea pot and cups
LYNN FISHER, artist
Route 2, Box 41
Bellaire, MI 49615

Plate (Peanut Butter and Jelly Sandwich)
POTTERY BARN
700 Broadway
New York, NY 10003

Children's artwork and toys
Special thanks to ALISSA TRZECIAK

CHAPTER 13 / CHOCOLATE LOVER'S TEA

Plate (Truffles)
DIANA WHITE

Tea set
SADLER AND CO.
225 5th Avenue
New York, NY 10001

CHAPTER 14 / FEEL BETTER TEA

Bedding (quilt, pillowcase, and ruffled pillow)
SHERIDAN
595 Madison Avenue
New York, NY 10022

Bed tray
WICKERY
342 3rd Avenue
New York, NY 10010

Honey jar and glass bowl (Preserves)
WOODEN INDIAN ANTIQUES
60 West 15 Street
New York, NY 10011

Vase, teapot, tea cup and saucer, silver toast holder
H. LEXINGTON COLLECTION
907 Madison Avenue
New York, NY 10021

CHAPTER 15 / LATE - NIGHT TEA

Teapot, sandwich plate, candlesticks, and pedestal plate
H. LEXINGTON COLLECTION
907 Madison Avenue
New York, NY 10021

Vase
MILLER ROGASKA
225 5th Avenue
New York, NY 10001

CHAPTER 16 / BARE BONES TEA

All props from private collections.

ENDPAPERS

BRUNSCHWIG & FILS
75 Virginia Road
North White Plains, NY 10603

INDEX

Alice Paradis' Peach Preserves, 27
Almond Cakes, 91
Almond mocha cake, 66–67

Baby Shrimp with Cashews, 87
Bacon, in tarts, 58–59
Bananas, in peanut butter sandwiches, 121
Basil mayonnaise, 60
Biscuits, for chicken sandwiches, 44
Black Forest Ham Sandwiches, 64
Black tea, 12, 13
Blinis with Caviar and Sour Cream, 78–79
Boiled Frosting, 49
Buttercream Frosting, 99

Cajun Shrimp Sandwiches, 45
Cake
    almond, 91
    almond mocha, 66–67
    carrot egg, 74
    chocolate, 98, 104–105
    coconut, 48–49
    dark chocolate, 104–105
    easy yellow, 98
    gingerbread, 60
    ice cream cone, 98–99
    lemon bundt, 41
    poppy seed, 112
    Russian spice, 82
    sponge, 35
    tea, 82
California Chicken Sandwiches, 112
Carrot Egg Cake, 74
Cashews, shrimp with, 87
Caviar, blinis with sour cream and, 78–79
Cheese
    cream cheese frosting, 74
    goat cheese tartlets, 39
    grilled cheese sandwiches, 119

prosciutto and explorateur sandwiches, 102
    Roquefort, Walnut, and Cognac sandwiches, 32
    Stilton, walnut, and pear sandwiches, 65
Cheese Tart Shells, 58
Chicken
    clove puffs, 70
    fried, in biscuit sandwiches, 44–45
    fried nuggets, 45
    liver pâté, 72
    in peanut sauce, 88
    sandwiches, 38, 102, 112
Chicken Consommé, 108
Chocolate cake, 98
Chocolate Chip Scones, 103
Chocolate Delight Cake, 104–105
Chocolate Dipped Shortbread Hearts, 103
Chocolate-Dipped Strawberries, 72
Chocolate Ganache, 105
Chocolate Truffles, 105
Chutney, 53, 102
Cinnamon Rolls, 80–81
Cinnamon Toast Fingers, 120
Classic Sponge Cake, 35
Clotted Cream, 26
Clove Chicken Puffs, 70
Clove-Studded Lemon Wedges, 26
Cobbler, 55
Coconut Cake, 48–49
Cookies
    chocolate-dipped shortbread hearts, 103
    Christmas, 66
    ginger snaps, 41
    sour cream sugar, 49
    toll house, 96
    Welsh currant, 26
Cranberry Scones, 60
Cream Cheese Frosting, 74
Creamed Mushrooms, 118
Cream of Tomato Soup, 114

Cream puff shells, 70
Cream Scones, 96
Crepes, 121
Crescent Moon Melon Slices, 88
Cucumbers and Sour Cream, 79
Cucumber Sandwiches, 30, 64
Currants, in cookies, 26
Currant Scones, 32
Curried Egg-Mayonnaise Sandwiches, 30
Curried Tuna Salad Sandwiches, 40
Custard, 41

Dark Chocolate Cake, 104–105
Date-Nut Scones, 73
Decaffeinated tea, 15
Deviled Eggs, 71
Dill, Salmon sandwiches with, 30
Dressing
    for clove chicken salad, 70
    red cabbage and bacon vinaigrette, 58

Easy Crepes, 121
Easy Yellow Cake, 98
Egg Mayonnaise and Watercress Sandwiches, 64
Eggs
    in carrot cake, 74
    curried egg salad, 70
    deviled, 71
    herb omelet, 121
    on toast, 108

Fabergé Carrot Cake, 74
Filled Chinese Pancakes, 86–88
Fish
    curried tuna salad sandwiches, 40
    salmon sandwiches, 30, 79
Fresh Sliced Fruit, 115
Fried Chicken 'N' Biscuit Sandwiches, 44–45
Fried Chicken Nuggets, 45

Frosting
    for almond mocha cake, 66–67
    buttercream, 99
    for coconut cake, 49
    cream cheese, 74
    two-cream, 82
Fruit
    sliced, 115
    white chocolate dipped, 105
Fruit and Nut Scones, 66
Fruit Butters, 27
Fruit Sauce, 61
Fruit Tarts, 34

Gingerbread, 60
Ginger Snaps, 41
Goat Cheese and Sun-Dried Tomato
    Tartlets, 39
Grandma Paradis' Quickie Chocolate Cake,
    98
Green tea, 12, 14
Grilled Cheese Sandwiches, 119

Ham Sandwiches, 96
Ham Salad in Corn Muffin Cups, 46
Herbal tea, 15, 17
Herb Omelet, 121
Horseradish sauce, 38
Hot Buttered Toast, 108

Ice Cream Cone Cakes, 98–99
Iced tea, 16, 17

Jam
    strawberry, 27
    toast points with, 118
Jane Mudry's Christmas Cookies, 66
Judie's Lemon Curd, 34

Lemonade Tea, 17
Lemon bundt cake, 41

Lemon Crisps, 73
Lemon curd, 34
Lemon wedges, 26

Maggie Barry's Half-Pound Poppy Seed
    Cake, 112
Mary's Almond Mocha Cake, 66–67
Mayonnaise
    curried-egg, 30
    turkey sandwiches with basil, 60
    watercress sandwiches with egg, 64
Meat
    bacon and red cabbage vinaigrette tarts,
        58–59
    ham salad, 46
    ham sandwiches, 64, 96
    prosciutto sandwiches, 102
    roast beef sandwiches, 38
    shepherd's pie, 52–53
Melon, 88
Miniature Cream Puff Shells, 70
Miniature Pita Pizzas, 94
Mint Tea Juleps, 17
Mocha almond cake, 66–67
Muffins, 46
Mushrooms, 118

Nuts
    date-nut scones, 73
    and fruit scones, 66
    See also specific nuts.

Omelet, 121
Onions, in raisin chutney, 53
Oolong tea, 12, 14
Orange pekoe tea, 14

Pancakes, Chinese, 86–88
Pastries
    cinnamon rolls, 80–81
    dough, 34

lemon wedges, 26
    Scottish petticoat tails, 32
Pâté, chicken liver, 72
Peach preserves, 27
Peanut Butter and Banana Sandwiches, 121
Peanut Butter and Jelly Sandwiches, 95
Peanut sauce, chicken in, 88
Pears, in sandwiches, 65
Pecan Scones, 49
Pita pizzas, 94
Poppy seed cake, 112
Potato Salad in Cucumber Compotes, 46
Preserves
    peach, 27
    Russian tea with sour cherry, 81
Prosciutto and Explorateur Cheese
    Sandwiches, 102

Raisin and Onion Chutney, 53
Red Cabbage and Bacon Vinaigrette Tarts,
    58–59
Red Egg on Toast, 108
Renny White's Biscuits, 44
Roast Beef Sandwiches with Horseradish
    Sauce, 38
Rolls, 80–81
Roquefort, Walnut, and Cognac
    Sandwiches, 32
Russian Spice Cake, 82
Russian Tea with Sour Cherry Preserves, 81

Salad
    clove chicken, 70
    ham, 46
    potato, in cucumber compote, 46
Sandwiches
    Cajun shrimp, 45
    chicken, 38, 44–45, 102, 112
    cucumber, 30, 64
    curried egg-mayonnaise, 30
    curried tuna salad, 40

grilled cheese, 119
ham, 64, 96
peanut butter and banana, 121
peanut butter and jelly, 95
prosciutto and explorateur cheese, 102
roast beef with horseradish sauce, 38
Roquefort, walnut, and Cognac, 32
salmon, 30, 79
Stilton, walnut, and pear, 65
turkey, 59, 60, 102
watercress, 64, 72
Sauces
    fruit, 61
    horseradish, 38
    peanut, 88
Sautéed Chinese Vegetables, 88
Scones
    chocolate chip, 103
    cranberry, 60
    cream, 96
    currant, 32
    date-nut, 73
    fruit and nut, 66
    pecan, 49
    walnut, 40
Scottish Petticoat Tails, 32
Shells
    for cheese tarts, 58
    miniature cream puff, 70
    for tartlets, 39
Shepherd's Pie, 52–53
    Shredded Chicken in Peanut Sauce, 88
Shrimp
    with cashews, 87
    sandwiches, 45
Sliced Chicken Sandwiches, 102
Smoked Salmon and Dill Sandwiches, 30
Smoked Salmon Sandwiches on Dark
    Bread, 79
Smoked Turkey and Chutney Sandwiches,
    102

Soup
    chicken consommé, 108
    tomato, 114
Sour cherry preserves, Russian tea with, 81
Sour cream
    blinis with caviar and, 78–79
    cucumbers with, 79
    in sugar cookies, 49
Sour Cream Sugar Cookies, 49
Spice cake, 82
Sponge cake, 35
Stilton, Walnut, and Pear Sandwiches, 65
Strawberries, chocolate-dipped, 72
Strawberry Jam, 27
Strawberry-Raspberry Cobbler, 55
Stuffing, in turkey sandwiches, 59
Sugar cookies, sour cream in, 49
Sun-Brewed Iced Tea, 17
Sweet and Crunchy Walnuts, 91
Sweet Pastry, 34

Tangy Lemon Bundt Cake, 41
Tarts
    bacon and red cabbage vinaigrette, 58–59
    fruit, 34
    goat cheese and sun-dried tomatoes, 39
    vanilla custard fruit, 41
Tea
    brewed, 23–24
    decaffeinated, 15
    growth areas, 12–13
    herbal, 15, 17
    iced, 16
    introduction to America, 12
    lemonade, 17
    perfect cup or pot, 16
    Russian with sour cherry preserves, 81
    sun-brewed iced, 17
    types, 12–15
Tea service
    serving tea, 23–24

tea basics, 23
tea food service, 20–21, 25
Tea bags, 25
Tea Cakes, 82
Timothy's Chicken Liver Pâté on Toast
    Rounds, 72
Toast
    chicken liver pâté on, 72
    cinnamon, 120
    hot buttered, 108
    red egg on, 108
Toast Points with Jam, 118
Toll House Cookies, 96
Tomatoes, sun-dried, 39
Tomato soup, 114
Truffles, 105
Turkey sandwiches, with chutney, 102
Turkey and Stuffing Sandwiches, 59
Turkey Sandwiches with Basil Mayonnaise,
    60
Two-Cream Frosting, 82

Vanilla Custard Fruit Tarts, 41
Vegetables, sauteed Chinese, 88
Vinaigrette, red cabbage and bacon, 58

Waldorf Chicken Salad Sandwiches, 38
Walnuts
    in Roquefort and Cognac sandwiches, 32
    and Stilton and pear sandwiches, 65
    sweet and crunchy, 91
Walnut Scones, 40
Watercress Sandwiches, 64, 72
Welsh Currant Cookies, 26
"Whatever" Croques, 120–121
White Chocolate Dipped Fruit, 105

Yellow cake, 98